FREEDOM ON TRIAL

The war against Palestine and the
fight for justice in America,
a memoir of the L.A. Eight and civil rights,
and the battle against being branded as "Terrorists".

MICHEL SHEHADEH

1st edition 2026

ISBN Paperback: 978-1-970487-13-8
ISBN Hardcover: 978-1-970487-14-5
LCCN: 2026904886
Printed in the United States of America
For permissions or inquiries:
www.michelshehadeh.com
michelshehadeh56@gmail.com

Publisher:
Bridge Publisher
www.bridgepublisher.com

Advance Praise for Freedom on Trial

Freedom on Trial is a powerful account of the case of the Los Angeles Eight, revealing how the state wields claims of "national security" to criminalize dissent and silence immigrant voices, particularly those advocating for Palestinian liberation. Michel Shehadeh's story reminds us that the defense of civil liberties here cannot be separated from the struggle for justice everywhere.

Angela Davis,
Distinguished Professor Emerita, Political Activist, and Author

With Palestine at the center of global consciousness, Michel Shehadeh's story is a searing warning—and a portrait of steadfast resolve. He exposes how a system built on repression and propaganda normalizes atrocity, obscures the human cost of U.S. imperialism, and paves the way for genocide. Like so many Palestinians, Shehadeh's only "crime" was the desire for self-determination. Yet this is also the account of a fight that was fought and won, carrying a crucial lesson for younger activists: that resistance, persistence, and principled struggle can prevail. His account is essential reading—this injustice won't stop unless we tie Palestinian liberation to our own.

Abby Martin,
Journalist, Filmmaker, and Founder of The Empire Files

As Palestinian voices face renewed repression today, Freedom on Trial reveals how the L.A. Eight survived surveillance, prosecution, and deportation threats for speaking the truth decades earlier. Their courageous 20-year fight—told brilliantly by Michel Shehadeh—reshaped immigrant rights and delivers a powerful lesson for our time: repression can and must be exposed, resisted, and defeated. Free Palestine!

Medea Benjamin,
Cofounder, CODEPINK

I came to Freedom on Trial by Michel Shehadeh not as a reader of history, but as someone living its continuation. I did not know the full story of the

L.A. 8 before my arrest, but it was the first thing my lawyer told me upon detention, a reminder that what I was facing had been done before. In these pages, Michel Shehadeh exposes how the U.S. government has long used immigration law to punish Palestinian speech. I recognized the same tactics, the same logic, the same attempt to silence Palestinian voices through law and fear. This book is not history alone; it is a living guide for those of us still fighting today.

Mahmoud Khalil, USA

Freedom on Trial tells the remarkable story of the Los Angeles Eight case—one of the longest and most consequential political deportation battles in U.S. history. As one of their lead attorneys, I witnessed firsthand the courage and resilience of Michel Shehadeh and his fellow respondents as they confronted a government determined to silence their political beliefs and suppress the Palestinian narrative they sought to share. Michel's account captures both the human cost of that struggle and the profound constitutional questions it raised about free speech and the rights of immigrants in America. This powerful book reminds us that the defense of civil liberties—and the right to tell one's own story—is never abstract; it is lived, fought for, and won by those willing to stand their ground.

Marc Van Der Hout
Lead Counsel for the Los Angeles Eight,
Former National President,
National Lawyers Guild

Freedom on Trial recounts the foundational chapter in the struggle over the Palestinian narrative within the American consciousness, beginning with the "Los Angeles Eight" case in 1987—one of the longest political deportation trials in U.S. history. Michel Shehadeh offers not merely a personal memoir, but a documentation of a broader battle for awareness waged by Palestinians in the West, culminating decades later in Palestine becoming a decisive factor in American politics. This book is both testimony and resistance—a pivotal chapter in the struggle between narrative and justice.

Nasser Kandil,
Editor-in-Chief of the Lebanese newspaper Al-Binaa,

Freedom On Trial is a powerful excavation of one of the most shameful chapters in America's modern history—a time when Palestinian identity and political dissent were criminalized in the name of national security. Michel Shehadeh's own account, as one of the L.A. Eight exposes how fear, surveillance, and racialized suspicion were weaponized to silence solidarity with Palestine. This book is not only a historical record—it is a mirror reflecting the ongoing struggle for justice, voice, and belonging. With piercing clarity and moral conviction, Michel Shehadeh exposes the architecture of repression built to criminalize Palestinian activism in America. The story of the L.A. Eight is a blueprint of how dissent is targeted, surveilled, and vilified—and a call to resist these patterns wherever they reappear. This book is both testimony and warning: the struggle for Palestine and the struggle for justice in America are inseparable."

Michel Shehadeh's 'Freedom on Trial' is a sweeping, deeply human memoir of courage, family, and the firm pursuit of justice. This is a story of survival without bitterness, resistance without hatred, and hope that refuses to die. A moving testament to resilience, love, family, and truth, no matter how long suppressed, will always rise. A riveting account of survival, renewal, and the enduring power of hope.

It began with a child's whisper,
and ended with the state pounding at my door.

To my sons, my grandchildren, and my wife; to my comrades in the
Los Angeles Eight; and to all who stand with Palestine, may our
struggle forever blossom into justice and freedom.

Contents

Foreword

Nearly forty years ago, immigration officials in Los Angeles arrested eight young immigrants—seven Palestinian men and the wife of one of them, a Kenyan. The immigrants were mostly students. Two were permanent residents; the others were on student visas. They were not charged with any criminal activity whatsoever, but they had been involved in pro-Palestinian activism. The government charged them all with being associated with a group that advocated the doctrines of world Communism, a justification for deportation dating back to the McCarran-Walter Act of 1952, a Cold War relic. What ensued was a 21-year battle for the rights of immigrants and the future of the eight immigrants.

I agreed to join the team representing the group, which became known as the L.A. Eight. At the time, I was one of the few practicing attorneys in the country with experience defending a communist deportation case. (This was, after all, the nineteen-eighties, not the nineteen-fifties.) The local lawyers on the case reached out to me because I had recently represented someone else facing similar charges-the writer Margaret Randall, a U.S.-born citizen who had obtained Mexican citizenship while married to a Mexican poet, thereby losing her American citizenship, according to the U.S. government. In 1984, after their divorce, she returned to the United States, got remarried, and applied for permanent residency in America. The government denied the application and sought to deport her under the McCarran-Walter Act, arguing that her writings—she was a prolific author of oral histories, journals, and poetry—advocated the doctrines of world Communism. After a trial in which Randall was cross-examined about a literary magazine that she co-edited and a piece of writing in which she praised her three-year-old son for becoming "communist" as he had learned to share his toys, an immigration judge ordered that she be deported. But we won the case on appeal when the Board of Immigration Appeals ruled that Randall had not, in fact, lost her U.S. citizenship when she became a Mexican citizen. As a U.S. citizen, she could not be deported, no matter how many "doctrines of world Communism" she advocated.

The arrests of the L.A. Eight, on a similar charge, with which Michel Shehadeh, one of the eight, opens this memoir, followed a three-year F.B.I. investigation that had begun as the city prepared to host the 1984 Olympics. Looking for potential terrorist threats, the F.B.I. identified a group of young Palestinian activists. F.B.I. agents reported on their teach-ins and protests, monitored the literature they distributed, recorded license plates of individuals who attended their meetings, surveilled the activists for extended periods, and sent at least one undercover agent to attend a haflis, or annual public community dinner, that the group helped organize. The agent's report stated that although he could not speak Arabic, it was clear from the tone of the music and the speeches that the event was a fundraiser for terrorism. Ultimately, as the F.B.I. director at the time, William Webster, testified, the Bureau concluded that the individuals had committed no crimes, let alone terrorism.

But the F.B.I. nonetheless urged immigration authorities to deport them, not because they had engaged in any criminal activity but because they were effective activists. The F.B.I. characterized the group's protests as "anti-Israel" and "anti-Reagan." The agents singled out Khader Musa Hamide, a green-card holder, whom they described as the group's ringleader, because he was "intelligent, aggressive, dedicated, and shows great leadership ability." Michel's story, which unfolds in the pages that follow, begins with the harrowing morning of his arrest, as he was forcibly separated from his wife and child in the early morning hours, and locked up as a grave threat to our national security.

Michel and his friends were held in maximum security for nearly a month. But ultimately, an immigration judge ordered their release when the government refused to disclose the evidence that it claimed showed that they posed a threat to national security. If the government would not give the detainees a fair chance to confront and rebut the evidence, the judge ruled, she would not consider it. At that point, in the absence of any admissible evidence that they posed any threat to anyone, the judge ordered their release. But their case was only beginning. They were free, but they still faced deportation charges for their "communist" associations.

We challenged the constitutionality of the "world Communism" deportation provision, and in 1989, a federal court declared that the provision was unconstitutional. The court ruled that the First Amendment protects all persons in the United States, including noncitizens. Since a citizen could not be punished for advocating world Communism, a noncitizen could not be deported for that reason. In our argument, we relied on a 1978 Supreme Court case, First National Bank v. Bellotti, that had extended First Amendment protections to corporations. The Court had reasoned that the First Amendment by its literal terms protects "speech," not particular speakers, and does so in the interest of insuring a robust public debate for listeners, regardless of the source of any specific speech. Corporations have speech rights, the Court maintained, because we all have an interest in the speech they create. If corporations have First Amendment protection for that reason, we argued, surely noncitizens do, too. The district court in L.A. agreed, and Congress in 1990 repealed the "world Communism" deportation provision that

But the case continued in immigration court. Congress enacted a new law rendering those who provide "material support" to a terrorist organization deportable, and the government amended its charges to include that provision. We objected that this was unconstitutional "selective prosecution," and federal courts blocked the deportations for many years, finding that our clients had been impermissibly singled out for their political speech and associations, while noncitizens supporting the Contras in Nicaragua and the Mujahideen in Afghanistan were not deported. Selective prosecution based on constitutionally impermissible reasons, such as speech or race, has long violated the Constitution.

That victory led Congress to amend the immigration law again, seeking to bar federal courts from barring the enforcement of immigration laws. The lower federal courts ruled that this new law did not apply to our case, but the Supreme Court eventually reversed, ruling in 1999 that the new law barred federal court intervention, and that the selective prosecution defense isn't applicable to an immigration case.

Still, the case that would not die was not over. The Supreme Court returned the case to immigration court, where finally, in 2007, the immigration judge dismissed the case for prosecutorial misconduct, calling the case "an embarrassment to the rule of law." The George W. Bush Administration declined to pursue an appeal. While the case was pending, the L.A. Eight grew older, some married and had children, and some became citizens. They have worked in affordable housing, civil engineering, construction, and the food industry, among other jobs. They had to spend more than two decades defending their right to remain here simply because they advocated for Palestinian self-determination.

Michel Shehadeh's memoir tells the important story of what it was like fighting for two decades, not just to remain in the United States, but to vindicate the speech rights of noncitizens while insisting on his own right to advocate for Palestinian self-determination. It's a harrowing story, powerfully told as only one who has lived it can tell. For Michel and his colleagues, it meant years of uncertainty, stress, and limitation on their ability to see their relatives in Palestine. (Any departure risked being treated as an abandonment of their fight to remain, so they were ironically compelled to stay here for two decades in order to win the right to stay here permanently.) But for all the pain and suffering it caused, Michel's saga did, for a considerable period, put an end to efforts to deport immigrants for mere speech. By fighting for his rights, he vindicated the rights of all immigrants.

Until now, Michel's story is suddenly more relevant than ever, as the Donald Trump administration revives the tactics used against Michel and his friends several decades ago. Thus, when Homeland Security agents arrested the Columbia graduate student Mahmoud Khalil for his role in leading pro-Palestine protests at the university, the arguments seemed eerily familiar. As Michel and another of the L.A. Eight did, Khalil holds a green card, authorizing him to remain here permanently. Like those activists, he is accused of leading protests with which the government disagrees. And, as with the L.A. Eight, the government argues that it can punish him for speech that would plainly be constitutionally protected for a U.S. citizen. The White House press secretary claims that Khalil "organized group protests" and "distributed pro-Hamas propaganda." Donald Trump posted on Truth Social that his Administration would seek to deport anyone engaged in "pro-terrorist, anti-Semitic, anti-American activity."

But the First Amendment protects the right to protest, to distribute pro-Hamas literature, and even to make "pro-terrorist, anti-Semitic, and anti-American" statements. The Court has held that it protects the right of the Klan to burn crosses and call for revenge against African Americans, the right of Nazis to march in Skokie, Illinois, and the right to burn an American flag.

In Khalil's case and that of several other Palestinian activists, the Administration has invoked a little-used immigration law empowering the Secretary of State to order the deportation of any noncitizen whose "presence or activities" would have "serious adverse foreign policy consequences." That provision was designed with high-level diplomats in mind, such as when the government is deciding whether to give a visa to a political leader charged with war crimes. The notion that pro-Palestine protests on a single college campus have "serious adverse foreign policy consequences" is absurd on its face. If that were the case, the United States could deport literally thousands of students across the country who participated in protests of the war in Israel and Gaza. And allowing deportation in these circumstances would be unconstitutional, for it would violate what the Supreme Court has called the "bedrock principle" of the First Amendment: "that the government may not prohibit the expression of an idea simply because society finds the idea itself offensive or disagreeable." Michel's case helped establish the principle that principle brooks no discernible distinction between citizens and noncitizens who live among us.

— David Cole

This foreword is adapted by the author from his article, "The Last Time Pro-Palestinian Activists Faced Deportation," The New Yorker, March 18, 2025.

Preface

When the case of the L.A. Eight finally came to an end, I thought:

Now, I can breathe.

For twenty years, I had lived under siege: accused, surveilled, silenced. All I wanted was to move on, to laugh without caution, to dream without fear, and to build the life I had postponed.

The case consumed the most vital years of my life, years meant for building a career, raising children, and growing as a person. Instead, I faced constant uncertainty, legal battles, and the fear of deportation. I longed to escape this burden, but the world, my community, and my conscience would not let me.

Friends, comrades, and fellow activists urged me to write this book. They reminded me that our story was not just mine; it was the story of every immigrant targeted for their beliefs, every Arab and Muslim who had felt the sting of suspicion, and every person who dared to dissent.

At first, I resisted. I did not want to reopen old wounds or make my family relive the pain. But memory calls us back, and history teaches us that silence can be a form of betrayal. So I began to write, slowly, cautiously. What I found was that writing this story was not only emotionally demanding, but also intellectually overwhelming. How do you capture twenty years of struggle that spanned legal complexities, shifting political climates, and deeply personal moments?

This memoir is my story, told as I remember it. The other seven who endured this case with me appear only as I knew and experienced them, always with respect, as part of the larger truth we carried together.

Writing this story meant balancing the personal and the political, the intimate and the legal. How do you convey something so deeply personal while also addressing the broader historical and political context? The L.A. Eight case unfolded during pivotal moments: 9/11, the Oslo Accords, the fall of the Soviet Union, and more. These events shaped our case and the legal tools used to target us. I could not untangle the personal from the political, so I chose to weave them together, truthfully, honestly, and imperfectly.

As I wrote, the urgency of telling this story became clear. The case of Mahmoud Khalil, a Palestinian student arrested for his activism, reminded me that the machinery of repression is still operational. The tactics may change, but the objective remains the same: to silence, erase, and break those who stand for Palestine.

This book is a resistance, a reclaiming of our narrative. It is not just about the L.A. Eight; it is about survival, defiance, and dignity. This story belongs to all of us. The case was not just a legal battle; it was about my family, my education, my exile, my right to stay, to be seen, and to be heard.

If you feel, as you read, like you are on a roller coaster, that is because that is exactly what it was. This story moves between heart and mind, between memory and history, between rage and resilience. It is a map, a warning, a chronicle of what repression looks like, and how it can be resisted.

I wrote this book for the record, for the struggle, for my family, for the future. For the communities that never stopped believing. For Mahmoud Khalil. For Palestine.

And I wrote it to say, simply and firmly: we were here. We fought. We endured. We never gave up.

This is our story. And now, it is yours.

Acknowledgements

I carry deep gratitude in my heart for those who gave me strength and courage throughout this journey.

To Professor Sherna Gluck, whose wisdom, encouragement, and countless hours of conversation helped me find clarity when the weight of memory felt too heavy.

To my friend Karim Boris, whose professional insight and thoughtful feedback enriched this book.

To our attorneys: David Cole, who guided us, offered generous feedback on this manuscript, and stood before the Supreme Court in our defense; Marc Van Der Hout, our tireless lead counsel; Ahilan Arulanantham, a distinguished lawyer and friend; the brilliant and legendary late Leonard Weinglass; the principled U.S. Attorney General, the late Ramsey Clark; the gifted Mark Rosenbaum; and the many others who defended us pro bono. I extend my deepest appreciation. Your commitment to justice carried us through our darkest years.

To attorneys Brian Hudson and Tony Hall, whose steadfast leadership in creating and guiding the Committee for Justice gave this struggle its anchor; and to the countless volunteers who demonstrated, came to court, wrote letters, and called Congress, you were the heartbeat of our defense.

I am also grateful to the judges who ruled with conscience, and to the organizations whose extraordinary support lifted us: the Center for Constitutional Rights (CCR), the National Lawyers Guild (NLG), the American Civil Liberties Union (ACLU), and the American Friends Service Committee (AFSC), as well as the many political and community organizations that stood by our side from beginning to end.

Finally, to my beloved family, who carried this burden with me, and to the children of Palestine, whose future we struggle for, I offer my enduring love and gratitude.

May our sacrifices sow the seeds of justice, until every child inherits freedom, dignity, and peace.

CHAPTER ONE

A RUDE AWAKENING

"Daddy," my three-year-old son Ibrahim whispered, his small head resting against my shoulder. His big brown eyes met mine, his wavy ash-brown hair tickling my ear as he clung to me.

"Can I sleep in your bed tonight?" he asked, his voice soft with hope.

I wanted to say yes. But I forced myself to shake my head. "No," I replied gently. "Big boys sleep in their own beds now."

I saw the doubt in his eyes, and I knew this had become a habit we needed to break. But as he glanced toward the window, I wondered if something else was on his mind.

"Are you scared?" I asked. He shook his head. "No."

Still, he tried again. "Can I come kiss you good morning?" I smiled, pulling him into a hug.

"Of course," I whispered, tucking him back into his bed and kissing him goodnight.

Maxine had an early morning. I, for once, had nothing to do. Just the rare luxury of sleeping in.

But barely a few minutes later, a thunderous banging shattered the stillness.

I shot up, disoriented. Who the hell is knocking at this hour?

A glance at the clock, 7:00 a.m.

I stumbled to the door, irritated. Through the glass, I saw them: a man and a woman, both dressed in crisp white shirts and gray slacks, standing on my front step.

"We're from the Immigration and Naturalization Service," the man said. "We need to talk to you."

I blinked. INS? Here? That didn't make sense. Immigration didn't do house calls. Something felt off.

Before I could respond, a sudden shove sent me stumbling backward. More agents poured in, storming past me with alarming aggression.

"Where are the weapons? Where are the weapons?" They shouted, their hands firm on my arms, pulling me into a headlock that cut off my air.

Weapons? I gasped for breath, my pulse racing. This wasn't real. This was a mistake.

Ibrahim appeared at the edge of the room, his eyes wide with terror, searching for me. One of the agents grabbed him roughly, tossing him onto the couch as though he weighed nothing.

Something inside me snapped. A surge of primal rage coursed through my veins, but the agent's grip around my neck tightened.

"Don't be stupid," the agent growled. "You don't want your son to see you getting hurt."

I froze. Ibrahim's big brown eyes locked onto mine, filled with confusion and terror.

The world slowed as I realized I was powerless to protect him.

The cold steel of handcuffs clamped onto my wrists.

I clung to a faint hope that this was a mistake, that somehow, reason would prevail, and I could break through the layers of bureaucracy.

"Can anyone explain what's happening?" I asked, my voice steady, though my mind raced. Protect Ibrahim. Don't let them hurt him. Was this a mix-up? A drug raid gone wrong? Why was I being treated like this?

The response came in a shrill, venom-laced voice: "You are under arrest!"

The agent in charge yanked a crumpled paper from his pocket and shoved it in my face, his glare burning with malice. "You belong to a terrorist organization."

Terrorist.

The word hit me like a slap. I froze. This wasn't a mistake. They were here for me. The grip on my neck tightened, the agent's breath hot against my skin.

I tried to process the accusation, terrorist? Was this because I was Palestinian? My crime was my identity.

For Palestinians, this moment isn't unfamiliar. We are always suspects. Always enemies. In the West, we are never seen as people. We're shadows, villains, threats, faceless monsters in the media.

The grip on my arms tightened, and the room grew suffocating. My mind spiraled, but one image stayed clear: my son's face.

Ibrahim's wide brown eyes locked onto mine, filled with confusion and terror. His tiny hands gripped the couch, his body trembling. He was silent, too silent. His fear was paralyzing.

This wasn't like a night away at daycare. He understood that something was terribly wrong.

His face, once filled with love and trust, now twisted in fear and betrayal. My heart shattered as I realized my son was watching his world fall apart, and I couldn't protect him.

"Let's go," the agent barked. They found nothing, no weapons, no explosives, just our everyday life. Yet they had come for us anyway, as if we were enemies.

Our lives were a constant balancing act, working full-time, attending school, and caring for our family. We weren't plotting attacks; we were struggling to make ends meet. Yet, in their eyes, we were threats. Not fathers. Not students. Not workers. But enemies. The absurdity of it was almost laughable. If only it wasn't so terrifying.

One of the agents noticed something on the coffee table, my Jordanian passport. It was a simple document, an afterthought I hadn't put away yet. To them, it might as well have been a weapon.

The agent snatched it and flipped through its pages, then passed it to his superior. Without a word, he pocketed it like a prize.

I barely reacted. The passport wasn't my concern. Then, they started pushing me toward the door.

A violent surge of resistance shot through me. "You can't leave my son alone in the house!" My voice cracked with desperation.

They didn't care. Ibrahim's terrified eyes, his little hands clenched, his chest rising and falling in rapid, terrified breaths, didn't matter. The weight of his innocence being ripped away hit me like a punch in the gut.

This wasn't supposed to happen in America.

I asked to call my wife. "Only one call," the agent said, voice sharp. I called her, steadying myself, telling her I was being arrested and to rush home for Ibrahim. The line went dead before I could reassure her.

She later told me that after the call, a lump lodged in her throat, and she couldn't speak. A coworker noticed her change, and she lied, "My husband needs urgent medical care." Then, she ran.

When the media covered the case later, they twisted her frantic escape into an excuse to fire her.

I turned back to the agents, pleading again. "Let's wait until my wife gets home." For a moment, hesitation flickered in their eyes.

Then, one agent sneered. "It seems we're giving him too many options."

And then, Ibrahim's voice cut through it all. "Where are you going, Daddy?"

I turned to see his tiny hands reaching out to me, as if his will could stop the nightmare. The storm of emotions inside me crashed, anger, helplessness, grief.

But above all, one thought consumed me: I was being taken away. And my son was watching.

I saw my neighbors' eyes, half-hidden behind doors and windows. They knew me. We'd shared meals, laughter, stories. But now, they stood silent witnesses to something that felt like a mistake too grotesque to believe.

I had once defended this government, argued that despite its flaws, it was still just, still worth believing in. Did I still believe that? I wasn't sure anymore.

Governments are run by people, some good, some bad. But a government itself? A machine, soulless, relentless, incapable of morality.

Through the chaos, a voice cut through.

"We'll take care of Ibrahim. Don't worry."

It was Kit, our immigrant Chinese neighbor. Her words, simple, steady, offered a sliver of hope amidst the madness. Ibrahim would be safe. He wouldn't be alone.

Kit and her husband ran a small store, a place where we had built quiet, steady friendships. It was a comfort to know Ibrahim would be with them until Maxine arrived.

But in the days that followed, my wife would feel the sting of the exception. One morning, the woman across the street, perhaps fueled by hysteria, spat at her as she left for work.

The venom in that act was raw and deliberate, but even she would come to regret it, later apologizing. Despite that, the scars remained. Ibrahim would take two years to recover from the trauma, nights drenched in sweat, waking in screams.

The scene outside was surreal. A grotesque spectacle meant to terrorize, not enforce justice. Squads of officers, armored and armed, sealed off the street. Flashing lights. A helicopter overhead. It didn't feel like Long Beach; it felt like a war zone.

I moved as if in a nightmare, the memories flooding back. I was no longer in California; I was back in Ramallah, under occupation. The same helicopters. The same soldiers. The same prisoners paraded as criminals.

But this wasn't the West Bank; it was Southern California. This wasn't supposed to happen here.

The government's theatrics painted a picture of a violent extremist, a terrorist mastermind. The truth? I was just a student. A father. An innocent man.

Michel Shehadeh with his three-year-old son Ibrahim, in 1987

The media coverage fed the hysteria: "Massive anti-terror raid nets dangerous Palestinian extremists." The headlines sensationalized the event, turning it into a spectacle of national security.

The reality? We were Palestinian refugees, new targets in America. We had been made the enemy by a system of fear and control.

At a community gathering later, I spoke about the agents' failure to read me my rights, an obvious violation. But one person in the crowd murmured, "No mistake was made; immigrants don't have rights."

The words hung heavy in the air. We already knew it. We just hadn't dared to say it aloud.

CHAPTER TWO

THE NIGHTMARE

The radio droned on about snow falling somewhere far away, a world that felt light-years from my own reality. I had no idea where they were taking me, but I couldn't focus on that. My mind raced with dark thoughts.

They'd seated me by the window. A cold thought gripped me: "It's easier to push me out from here." I forced myself to breathe, telling myself, "No, not in America. They don't do things like this." But then, the terror of the Mossad flashed through my mind; Palestinians disappear all the time. The fear was almost paralyzing.

I had read the stories. Yet, the spectacle of my arrest, the helicopters, the flashing lights, felt too public. It wasn't a covert operation. It wasn't a Mossad hit. But the result was the same, I was under arrest.

"Does it snow in Jordan?" the agent beside me asked, snapping me out of my thoughts. I ignored him.

"Lebanon gets snow, right?" he pressed, his voice casual but with something else hidden beneath.

I kept my silence, turning my attention to the blur of the road outside. This wasn't the time to speak, not now, not with everything I knew they would twist.

I remembered the America I had dreamed of, the endless possibilities, the freedom. But as I sat there, hands bound, I could no longer ignore the truth. The dream wasn't for people like me. It never had been.

The car jolted, throwing me back to the present. My mind, however, was still stuck with Ibrahim. Was he okay? Had my wife reached him yet? The questions gnawed at me with every streetlight we passed.

Outside, the city passed in cold, lifeless boxes of concrete and steel. They didn't look like homes. They didn't look like America.

In America, houses rose overnight, pre-designed, mass-produced, with climate control and modern comforts. Yet, they felt hollow, stripped of the warmth that makes a house a home. The warmth I longed for was not in these walls, but in the memories of my past.

In Palestine, homes were built over generations. A father would start small, adding rooms as his family grew, creating spaces that carried the history of those who lived within them. These homes were more than investments; they were roots, anchors to belonging.

But in America, homes were commodities, their value determined by market trends and appraisals, not by memories.

Was I beginning to understand the true meaning of roots, or was I simply retreating into nostalgia? Memory is selective. It softens hardship and amplifies innocence, laughter, and simpler times. Maybe that's how I coped with the ache of my lost homeland.

All immigrants carry their own myths of "back home," crafting romanticized versions of a past that may never have existed but feels more real than the present we navigate. I saw this in others, too. Each of us telling stories of home, painting our origins with longing instead of truth.

For Palestinians, this longing was deeper. We were not just immigrants, but exiles. We had lost not only a country but the right to return to it. Our homeland had been erased from the maps, renamed, redrawn by the ambitions of a settler-colonial project.

And yet, despite the grief, Palestinians built lives here. We raised families, contributed to society, and proved we belonged. We were no different from other immigrant communities, Latinos, Africans, Europeans, each carrying their past with them, unable to separate it from the present.

I could see it in my children. When they dismissed my "back home" lectures, I knew they would tell their own stories one day, too. Maybe not about Palestine, but about something lost, something remembered, something that only exists fully in hindsight.

Even now, when life feels overwhelming, I retreat into my memories, finding comfort in a time that feels untouched, unspoiled.

But suddenly, I was yanked back to reality. The hum of the FBI car, the tight grip of handcuffs, and the relentless stretch of the freeway ahead brought me back. The driver reached over and switched off the radio, leaving a deafening silence.

"When is this going to stop?" I thought bitterly. The heat inside the car felt suffocating, or perhaps it was my anxiety.

A fragment of conversation between the agents caught my attention:

"…I'll be going to New York…"

New York. The mention pulled me back in time, to 1975 when I had first arrived in America, fresh from Palestine. I landed in New York, my heart pounding with a mix of excitement and fear.

I had no destination. No contacts. Just a stranger in a city of strangers. I hailed a yellow cab, and the driver, an older Black man, turned to me.

"Where to?"

I hesitated, then said, "Take me to a reasonably priced hotel." He understood and dropped me off at a building I couldn't even name now.

In the hotel lobby, a sea of voices collided, but no one seemed to notice me. I felt invisible, yet the room was so full of life. I approached the front desk, feeling out of place, exposed.

I stayed in that cramped hotel room for five days, venturing out only for cheap food and short walks, too afraid to explore too far. I was lost in this city of skyscrapers and endless streets, disoriented by the number-filled address system and unable to use a payphone without getting confused.

Back home in Palestine, addresses were simple. A name, a town, nothing more. Here, everything seemed designed to keep me lost.

I could speak English, of course, but not like them. My accent was too heavy, and my words were often misunderstood. I repeated myself over and over, like an alien trying to communicate.

The feeling of being lost in a new world, both physically and mentally, was overwhelming. I wasn't just in a strange city; I was lost within myself.

The agent's voice cut through my thoughts, pulling me back to the present: "Do you want to say anything before we get there?"

I didn't respond. His attempt at casual conversation only intensified my resolve to remain silent. He pressed again, "You've been here a while. Talk about football if you want."

I kept silent, unwilling to give him anything. Finally, with impatience in his voice, he asked, "It's your last chance. Do you want to say anything?"

I let the silence hang for a moment before answering.

"Yes. Will I be able to contact a lawyer when we arrive?"

His smile vanished, replaced by anger. "You son of a bitch," he spat, slamming the door shut.

The car rolled into a dark parking lot at Parker Center, and the weight of isolation settled over me. Officers stood waiting, their eyes filled with suspicion, their posture rigid.

I was dragged through a dimly lit corridor, the flickering overhead lights casting shadows that seemed to stretch forever. I could only think: What have I done to deserve this?

CHAPTER THREE

IN THE BELLY OF THE BEAST

"More garbage?"

The cop at the counter smirked as the agents agreed.

I wanted to protest, to explain who I was, but I knew better. I stayed silent.

They led me through the building, past graffiti-covered walls and unknown doors. Weapons were casually stored in boxes as if it were just another day.

A buzzer sounded. A door opened. And I stepped into a hostile world.

Then, a familiar face, Ayman. What was he doing here? This wasn't his world. He wasn't meant for this.

I tried to signal him with my eyes, telling him not to be afraid, though I was telling myself the same thing. His vulnerability broke my heart.

Then they shoved me behind a plastic curtain, ordered me to strip, and inspected me. I complied, humiliated. By the time I was dressed, Ayman was gone.

I was placed in a glass-walled room, left with my thoughts. The raid. Ayman. None of it made sense. Then I saw more familiar faces, Ayman's brother Amjad, Naim Sharif, and Aiad Barakat. We were five now. Soon, we'd be eight.

I felt a surge of strength. I wasn't alone. Oddly, it comforted me.

Naim was across from me in another glass box, arguing with the same agent who had ridden in the car with me. He was furious, his body rigid with rage. I tried to signal him, don't talk to them without a lawyer. But he didn't listen.

Later, I asked him why. "I was furious," he said. "They arrested me at gunpoint in front of my three-year-old niece. She was terrified."

I understood. I would have done the same for Ibrahim.

An agent brought papers for me to sign, arrival confirmation, arrest time. Then I was left alone again in the glass box.

Isolation is cruel. It reminded me of my childhood, a different kind of exile. As a boy, I couldn't understand why I couldn't see my father. He was only an hour away in Amman, but I might as well have been on a different continent. The Israeli occupation created an invisible barrier between us.

Years later, I realized the cruelty was not just about politics; it was the deliberate isolation of people. Now, history was repeating itself. My son, Ibrahim, was just miles away, but I was locked away, unable to see or reassure him. The prison had changed, but the feeling was the same.

I was a son separated from my father. Now, I was a father separated from my son.

Suddenly, the door swung open.

"Out."

Still chained, I complied. They led me to a small room for fingerprinting. The agent pressed my inked fingers onto paper, treating me like a criminal.

Then, the door opened again. Khader Hamideh entered with another agent. For a fleeting moment, relief washed over me.

He was clean-shaven, wearing a dark jacket, looking professional. For a second, I thought he might be here to bail us out.

I smiled, hopeful, but his expression didn't match. He wasn't here to help us; he was one of us. A bitter laugh escaped me, realizing how deep this went.

Six of us were here now. Was this a mass arrest? My mind raced with questions I couldn't answer.

We were separated into glass-walled rooms, waiting for hours, then transferred to an immigration detention center. It was overcrowded, filled with men, mostly Mexican, Latino, and a few Asians. The air was thick with sweat, fear, and exhaustion.

We were together now, Amjad, Aiad, Ayman, Naim, Khader, and I. We huddled in the corner, sharing our stories of arrest, confusion, and helplessness. Then came the gnawing questions: Why we were here?

As the hours passed, others were processed and sent south, leaving just us. Aiad and Khader told us more bad news, Ghada, Aiad's wife, and her brother Haitham had been arrested too. Julie, Khader's wife, was also arrested. Later, we knew she was kept in custody at Sybil Brand Institute. They were accused of Visa violation.

Ghada and Haitham were released the next day. Meanwhile, the government escalated Julie's visa violation, linking her to our case as part of some fabricated conspiracy. In that moment, standing in the detention center, the fight for immigrant rights became personal.

We were all immigrants, hoping for a better life, yet here we were, treated as criminals. The idea of immigrant solidarity had never felt more real. No matter where we came from, we were now bound together, not just by chains, but by the shared struggle of being "the other."

The door burst open again. Officers stormed in, armed and armored. "Face the wall," they commanded. We complied, the weight of our restraints biting into our skin as they shackled us, wrists, waists, and legs, forcing our movements into unnatural steps.

We were prisoners, transported like criminals for nothing more than existing as Palestinians. The weight of it all, the physical, emotional, and psychological burden, was crushing.

CHAPTER FOUR

FACING THE SYSTEM

Upstairs, to our relief, Brian Hudson, our attorney and friend, was waiting. His presence immediately lifted our spirits. Even amid the chaos, he had acted swiftly, pulling together a defense team. At his side stood Tony Hall, a new ally. Together, they were the nucleus of our legal defense team. For the first time since the arrests, the heavy weight of isolation lifted, if only a little.

L.A. Eight attorney Tony Hall at a press conference

After greetings, our questions came fast. Brian raised his hand to steady us. "I know you have many questions," he said, his voice calm. "We don't know much yet."

He explained we would face a federal immigration judge soon, where the government would present charges and determine bail. He advised that we request a continuance to prepare a stronger case. We didn't like the idea of more waiting, but Brian reassured us: "Better to be prepared than to lose too quickly."

Tony Hall warned us: "The government wants to keep you in prison indefinitely. If we lose, you'll be stuck here much longer." Silence fell. Reality settled in. Tony softened. "A few more days here gives us time to build our case."

Shackled, we were led to Judge Thomas Y.K. Fong's courtroom. He was young, too young, I thought. Could he handle this high-stakes case?

The room was divided. On our side, six shackled men, Brian, Tony, and Gary Silbiger from the National Lawyers Guild. Our families were barred from attending, officially due to "lack of space." On the government side, INS prosecutor Melanie Fitzsimmons sat with her colleagues, flanked by armed guards.

I felt the weight of the moment. This was no routine hearing. This was the beginning of a long, brutal legal battle.

Fitzsimmons stepped forward, calm and calculated, clearly enjoying the moment. "Your Honor," she began, her voice cold, "the charges fall under the McCarran-Walter Act, Section 241(a)(6). It states that anyone affiliated with an organization advocating worldwide communism is deportable."

She paused, letting the words hang in the air. "They are dangerous people. They pose a national security risk. They are members of the Popular Front for the Liberation of Palestine." She took another dramatic pause. "This is a Marxist-Leninist international terrorist organization, designed to overthrow the U.S. and Israel."

Her voice rose, and my stomach clenched. This wasn't a scripted performance; it was my life. And the stakes were immense.

The McCarran-Walter Act, a relic of McCarthyism, was resurrected to target Palestinian activism. Fitzsimmons wielded it as a weapon to blur the lines between activism and terrorism. We denied the charges. We were innocent, yet we faced a government bent on silencing us.

Judge Fong's words were sharp. "These are serious charges, potentially involving national security endangerment." The media's frenzied coverage, including the Los Angeles Times headline, played directly into the government's hands. They wanted fear. They wanted us convicted in the court of public opinion before the trial even started.

Our attorneys requested more time to prepare, and Fitzsimmons, the INS prosecutor, didn't object. After all, keeping us locked up worked in their favor. The government's delay in serving the arrest papers only added to the absurdity. They filed them in mid-December but waited until late January, because they didn't want to disrupt holiday schedules.

Gary Silbiger, our attorney, pointed out, "If we're so dangerous, why were we left on the streets for weeks?"

But the government wasn't interested in logic. They were manufacturing fear. Judge Fong turned to us. "Anyone wish to remain in jail without bond?" We stood. Shackled, we remained still as the judge left. The next phase of this ordeal had begun.

Our attorneys were troubled, especially by Fong's casual remark about national security. We all hoped he wouldn't preside over the bond hearing. Later, a new judge, Ingrid Hrycenko, entered. She was sharp, decisive, someone we hoped could be fair.

She granted the continuance, giving our defense team more time to prepare. "You'll remain in custody until then," she said, and a date was set: February 17th.

The tension in the room thickened when INS Counsel Elizabeth Hacker stood to speak. "The government plans to present three to four witnesses to prove the respondents are a security risk."

Witnesses? A cold shiver ran through me. Who could they be? The idea of fabricated accusations, stories invented in their minds, filled me with rage. We weren't terrorists. We were just people trying to live.

As the hearing wrapped up, we were told there was a demonstration outside, led by Casey Kasem, the Arab American radio personality. People were standing with us. That brought a sliver of comfort, but our ordeal was far from over.

The FBI had planned a press conference to announce our arrests. After a delay, it was canceled, and a written statement was issued. The real reason was revealed: "Concern over American hostages in the Middle East." The government wasn't just targeting us; they were using us as bargaining chips.

The realization hit me hard. We weren't just political targets. We were prisoners in a game much bigger than us. The government had taken us in retaliation, treating us as pawns in a conflict we had no part in.

Shackled again, we were loaded into transport vans, heading for El Centro Prison. The officers, armed and cold, showed no signs of kindness. They regarded us not as men, but as threats, labels, not humans.

The journey was designed to humiliate, to make us feel like criminals. We were transported in metal cages, locked away like animals. The officers' glares pierced through the rearview mirror, filled with contempt. We were guilty in their eyes before the trial even began.

The spectacle was complete as the flashing lights of the escort vehicles surrounded us. To any onlooker, we were dangerous felons, but the truth didn't matter. After what seemed like hours, we finally arrived at El Centro Prison.

CHAPTER FIVE

COLD WALLS AND WARM SMILES
Brotherhood in Captivity

Inside El Centro Federal Detention Center, we were led into a cold, sterile reception area, where the ritual humiliation began again.

Another strip search. We were ordered to strip naked, no hesitation, no dignity. "Bend over. Cough." Contraband or no, it was clear: a declaration of power, a message: We own you now. When it was over, we were dragged to separate isolation cells on the tenth or twelfth floor.

The view through the tiny, barred window was bleak and unfamiliar. No food. No water. It felt deliberate, a methodical attempt to weaken and exhaust us. I fought to hold on to myself, but hunger gnawed, thirst scraped, and the body betrayed the mind.

At least I was alone. No cellmate to fear. I had read too many stories about horrors in U.S. jails. Isolation was better than the alternative.

Fatigue pressed into my bones, yet my mind raced. Endless "why?" questions circled in my head. Pacing the room, I ran my fingers along a small, rough wooden shelf, and then found it: a half-smoked cigarette, a single match, left behind for a desperate moment. I lit it and inhaled deep. For the first time since my arrest, I had control over something, even if it was just a single drag of stolen relief. The smoke curled toward the bright, unyielding prison light, twisting, stretching, comforting.

Sleep came in restless, fractured waves. Memories of my family, Ibrahim's voice, the relentless glare of light, they wouldn't let me fully escape. Eventually, a sudden noise jerked me awake, the clatter of footsteps, muffled voices, the mechanical hum of a world to which I didn't belong. No clocks marked the hours, just a sliver of sunlight through the narrow iron window.

Then, CLANK. The automatic door unlocked. A voice boomed over the loudspeaker: "Public time."

Disoriented, I forced myself up and stepped into the circular communal area, an alien world. Men drifted like shadows, some eating snacks from vending machines, others pacing, eyes distant. A few leaned against walls, smoking, observing. The air buzzed with whispered conversations, gestures, and the silent language of survival. Haggling, sizing each other up, it felt like another planet, with its own rules, its own currency of fear and favors.

This would be the last time we were allowed in a prison's public area. Soon, we would be isolated again, not just physically, but politically. The government's vilification machine was just beginning, crafting the narrative that would brand us as enemies.

Through the crowd, I spotted familiar faces, Amjad, Ayman, Aiad, Naim, and Khader. They were scanning the room, searching for me. And then we saw each other simultaneously. Faces lit up, hands shot up in greeting, smiles wide and genuine.

I hurried toward them, my own smile growing, heart pounding, not from fear, but from joy. We embraced tightly, a hug heavy with survival, brotherhood, and unspoken understanding. Ripped from our homes, branded as enemies, isolated in cold cells, but here we were, together.

And in that moment, nothing mattered more. They had saved me a chair, a silent gesture of solidarity, of belonging. I sat down, feeling as though I had won something priceless. Because I had.

In a place designed to break you, erase your sense of self, and make you feel utterly alone, we had found each other again, and that was everything. Isolation is cruel, emotionally draining, dulling the senses, eroding the spirit, making time lose its shape.

For the first time since our arrests, the suffocating weight of solitude lifted, if only briefly.

In the center of the space stood an elevated, circular glass-walled room, like a watchtower. Inside, guards moved casually, chatting, monitoring screens, projecting authority. Though it seemed relaxed, tension lingered. Everyone watched everyone. Prisoners watched guards; guards watched prisoners. Trust did not exist here. Danger had no uniform.

This prison was its own universe. Guards were untouchable overseers; prisoners existed only in the immediate, tangible moment, surviving, bargaining, scavenging. A cigarette, a piece of candy, a page from a magazine, these became currency, fragments of normalcy. Alcohol, drugs, news from the outside, coveted whispers of freedom in a place designed to erase it.

Prison life had its own unspoken rules. My prior notions, camaraderie, solidarity, and a shared struggle felt naive. I had imagined a Robben Island–type environment, Israeli jails under Apartheid, where imprisonment forged unity, where hunger strikes were declarations of dignity. But this was different. Here, selfishness thrived; survival meant preying on the weak. There was no battle for justice, only a battle against each other.

Reuniting with the others brought deep comfort, a reprieve from isolation. Faces I had known for so long now seemed new, kind, gentle, out of place in this hostile world. Silent gestures, a handshake, a pat on the back, a glance, became our quiet language: We're still here. We will get through this. Together. And together, we endured.

Amjad lightened the mood with silly jokes; Khader overanalyzed every detail, searching for patterns; Naim punctuated conversations with rhetorical questions and curses; Aiad spun conspiracy theories; Ayman worried aloud about his parents. I leaned into logic, feigning calm, trying to untangle our reality.

Despite fear and uncertainty, we found moments of laughter, sarcasm, and fleeting joy. These stolen moments were a quiet rebellion against despair. Shared anxiety, concern for our families, and unspoken understanding became the foundation of something stronger than fear, resilience.

We longed for the pocket money confiscated from us, a taste of normalcy, a fragment of control. Instead, we had only the dirty, sweat-soaked clothes from our arrest. Vending machines filled with snacks and bottled drinks taunted us. Hunger and thirst gnawed at us, turning cheap food into forbidden treasures. Cigarettes were especially vital for Aiad; without them and his coffee, he grew restless and irritable, pacing.

To distract ourselves, we spun endless theories. Why were we here? Who was behind this? What was coming next? But no answer satisfied.

This wasn't a maximum-security prison, but we had limited privileges, including access to public payphones for collect calls, a lifeline to the world outside, if anyone answered.

Amjad managed to reach his wife, Maria, married only a few days before our arrest. A typical Palestinian honeymoon, we joked darkly. In another life, they would have been escaping to a quiet seaside town, worried only about unpacking or dinner plans. But in Palestine, love and oppression are intertwined. Marriage is a declaration of survival, a defiance against forces that try to erase us.

Instead of soft mornings and stolen kisses, Amjad's first weeks of marriage were spent in shackles, Maria packing legal papers instead of suitcases. The first test of their love was enduring a government's attempt to shatter their lives before they'd begun.

Maria's voice carried worry and reassurance. "Big things are happening outside," she said carefully, unable to share more over the phone. "Everyone is working to get you out. You won't be in there for long." We clung to that hope, though doubt lurked in the shadows.

I tried calling Maxine, my wife. No answer. Again. Each failed call reminded me of our powerlessness, our isolation. But at least we had each other, our circle of comrades, a network of small but essential support. A joke, a theory, a pat on the back, these gestures made us stronger, prepared for whatever came next. The fear of separation remained, unspoken but real.

At the core, one truth persisted: we were innocent.

After two days in El Centro, the guards came for us again. Time in prison crawled, stretched, distorted. San Diego, once a city of sun, beaches, and freedom, now felt like a memory trapped behind iron bars. Each visit to familiar places, like Fairouz Café & Gallery, triggered reminders of confinement: gnawing hunger, vending machines stocked with forbidden treats, the ache of a lost normalcy.

The guards arrived unannounced. One by one, we were dragged out, still shackled, still treated as criminals in a script we hadn't written. We looked the part, disheveled, dirty, and exhausted. Denied showers, clean clothes, basic dignity, we slept in the same sweat-stiffened garments from our arrest.

The prison vans waited, doors open like the jaws of a beast. Flashing police cars flanked us, sirens screaming. To onlookers, we were a high-risk operation in motion, dangerous and monstrous.

But the truth was quiet, hidden in the back of those vans. We had no idea where we were going, no clue what awaited us. We were pawns in a game we didn't understand, moved without explanation.

As the convoy raced forward, my mind clung to one thought: this must be a mistake. Surely, the ordeal can't last. Surely, the truth will emerge. Surely, someone will see through the lies.

I closed my eyes, inhaled deeply, and reminded myself, we've done nothing wrong.

CHAPTER SIX

INSIDE MAXIMUM SECURITY
Life at Terminal Island

We arrived at a maximum-security section of the Terminal Island federal detention facility in San Pedro. This was to be our new residence.

The prison was infamous, known for corruption and bribery scandals in the early 1980s. A fortress designed not to rehabilitate, but to break men down.

For two hours, we had no idea where we were, exhausted, hungry, and disoriented. This wasn't the hunger of waiting for a meal; it was primal, uncontrollable. We begged. No one responded.

Finally, they threw us some food, dry bread, a few biscuits, two apples, and two oranges. We divided the scraps in silence, too drained to talk. Even small talk felt futile. I tried to nap, but sleep wouldn't come. We were all restless, waiting for something to make sense of this nightmare.

At 3 a.m., the guards returned for another invasive search, even more humiliating than the first. I was ordered to strip, bend over, and cough, just another display of their control. Afterward, they gave us blue uniforms, blankets, and canvas shoes.

We were shoved into separate cells, Naim and Amjad in one, Khader and Aiad in another, and Ayman and I in the middle. The doors slammed shut, metal against metal. Silence followed.

I stood with Ayman in our small, filthy cell. The oppressive silence felt oddly calming. For the first time in days, I wasn't being watched, and the absence of hostility was a strange relief.

Ayman and I sat on the bottom bunk. The last two days had been a whirlwind of humiliation. Each glance from a guard had been filled with contempt, as if our guilt was already decided.

But sitting there, I reminded myself that I had done nothing wrong. The wrongdoing was theirs, not mine. This thought gave me a small flicker of control, and I felt a slight shift in my mindset.

The cell was everything I had imagined, small, with a barred window that let in no light. A metal sink and a rusty toilet, both bolted to the wall. The bunk bed faced the locked door. By unspoken agreement, I took the bottom bunk, and Ayman took the top. We joked about it, pretending to visit each other's "rooms."

Over time, we gathered small items, toothpaste, and a few cigarettes. Ayman kept everything organized, while I constantly misplaced things. Even in this tiny space, I found myself asking, "Ayman, have you seen my...?"

The bathroom situation was the first challenge; privacy was impossible. We agreed to pretend to sleep whenever the other used the toilet. But over time, we grew comfortable enough to talk while one of us was on the toilet, creating our own sense of dignity in a place meant to strip it away.

The next morning, we were woken by a loud bang on the door.

"Wake up, camel jockeys!"

The guard's voice was sharp, followed by another taunt: "Eat your breakfast, sand n***s!" They had been waiting for us.

Primed with warnings of incoming "terrorists," the guards seemed to relish the opportunity for abuse. Their words weren't spontaneous; they were rehearsed. Even the "privileged" inmates joined in, following the lead of the system.

Terminal Island Federal Detention Facility in San Pedro, CA.

Eager to prove their loyalty, the guards parroted the insults, adding their own cruelty. The small hole in the cell door clanked open, and the food cart rolled down the corridor. A medium-built inmate with salt-and-pepper hair slid our trays through the slot, smirking as if playing a role in a Hollywood prison movie.

Breakfast was basic: a box of cereal, half a pint of milk, an overripe banana, and a plastic bowl with disposable cutlery. Alongside, we got a side of plastic and profanity, the two rulers of prison life. The guards controlled everything.

A small relief: the cell windows stayed open until food was delivered. Ayman leaned through, talking to others. When it was my turn, I did the same, catching brief glimpses of the outside world, a fleeting connection in our isolated existence.

I looked out to see heads sticking out from every door like figures frozen in time. Some talked eagerly, others just gazed, drinking in the small glimpse of life beyond. To my surprise, most were smiling, as if they'd escaped the suffocating confinement.

Then I spotted Aiad and Naim. Our eyes met, and the joy was immediate; words tumbled out in Arabic, a rush of excitement. For a few seconds, we reclaimed something they tried to take from us. But we knew it wouldn't last. Soon, the windows would shut, and we'd be sealed in again.

A strange thought flickered in my mind, those heads, poking out like horses in a stable, anticipating a small offering. The comparison hit me hard. I jerked back, retreating into the dim cell.

Ayman continued to engage, stretching the moment for as long as it would last. I sat, staring at the peeling walls, feeling the weight of the morning's slurs and the meager breakfast.

The guards had reduced us to animals, locked in cages of their making. Yet, Ayman's voice, still floating in the air, was a lifeline to the outside. I closed my eyes and let his words drift past, trying to ignore the bitterness.

Our immediate priority was communication. We weren't completely isolated, but the cell arrangement created a physical distance between us. Our collective strength had been severed, but we were determined to reclaim it.

We began knocking on the doors to speak, but the taps were hard to interpret, and others quickly grew annoyed. Some mocked us, imitating Arabic, turning our language into a cruel joke.

Then, one night, we heard Khader and Aiad's voices more clearly. We followed the sound, realizing that the pipes near the toilet carried the best sound. This discovery felt like a secret passageway, an act of defiance against the walls meant to break us.

Now, we could speak freely. The guards, the locked doors, and the watchful eyes couldn't silence us. But reaching Naim and Amjad was still a challenge. We found a partial solution with the inmates delivering supplies; some became our reluctant messengers.

The next day, we learned that we would get one hour of fresh air each day, from 4 p.m. to 5 p.m. It wasn't a privilege; it was a cruel reminder of what we had lost. Freedom had become a luxury, a brief brush of wind, and a sliver of sky.

We were segregated for that hour while the rest of the inmates remained locked away. They positioned us in adjoining basketball courts, separated by towering metal fences, and arranged us in the same formation enforced inside our cells—Ayman and I in the middle court. With nothing between us but steel mesh, we found a way to communicate.

Ayman and I became messengers, relaying messages between our cellmates. In the spare time we had, we exercised, not just to stay fit but to defy the system and remind ourselves that no matter what awaited us, we would face it standing strong.

Then came news, A reporter from the *Los Angeles Times* was visiting the next day. The mere name sparked a burst of energy. Perhaps this meant something. What we didn't know, but it felt like a crack in the darkness. For the first time in weeks, we had hope.

The next day, the reporter, Ronald Soble, arrived. We had already endured the same morning routine, a box of cereal, a glass of milk, and an overripe banana. The same cold, rationed sustenance.

We were told the interview would be conducted through a grimy door, barely opening. Soble's voice came through: "Can you tell me how you've been treated so far?" The question lingered.

I hesitated until Ayman nudged me forward. "Tell him how we're being treated like dogs." I took a deep breath and stepped forward.

"My name is Michel Shehadeh, and we are human beings, not animals," I declared, my voice steady.

As I spoke, my words gained power. "Is this America? Is this justice?" The words echoed through the room, challenging the system. But then something unexpected happened, other voices joined in, a wave of defiance. "IS THIS AMERICA? IS THIS JUSTICE?" The entire prison roared with anger and resilience.

The unity was electrifying. It was the first time we were heard. For those few moments, we weren't silent. The banging on doors, the shouting, it felt like solidarity. The guards panicked, and the interview was abruptly cut short. Soble was rushed out, leaving us with his parting words, "They've been here less than a week and already got the whole prison organized."

Back in our cells, we laughed, real laughter, something we hadn't felt in days. For once, we had made a statement. As the Arabic saying goes, "You cling to a straw to stay afloat."

The next morning, reality hit. "Get up, sand n***s!" The guards yelled, followed by taunts as they delivered our meager breakfast. Amjad rushed to the door, but hunger won over fury. We grabbed our trays and ate in silence.

In that moment, our minds wandered. We weren't in that cell; we were back home, thinking of labaneh, zaatar soaked in olive oil, scrambled eggs, hummus, and freshly baked bread. The taste of home felt distant in the cold, stale air of Terminal Island.

In prison, where even the smallest pleasures are stripped away, a cigarette becomes more than a vice. It's a form of resistance, a taste of normalcy, a moment of control.

But getting cigarettes? That was the real challenge. We pleaded with the guards to no avail. Deprivation, for an addict, is its own form of torture. So, we devised a plan, what did we have to bargain with? Noise.

That night, we banged on the door, shouting for cigarettes. The calm was shattered. Other inmates yelled at us to be quiet, but we didn't care. The guards rushed in, their faces filled with rage, threatening us with punishments. But we didn't stop. Finally, they caved.

One guard muttered, "I'll bring you some tobacco if you stop."

Ten minutes later, a guard returned with a small paper bag. "That's all we could come up with," he said, tossing it to Ayman. "Your friends got similar bags."

He slammed the window shut and left. Ayman and I stared at the bag, exchanging glances. We had expected cigarettes, at least a few loose ones, but instead, it was half-filled with dry, crumbling tobacco.

The smell was pungent and musty, the driest tobacco we had ever seen. But we were addicts, and logic didn't apply. We weren't about to turn it down.

Now came the next problem, how to smoke it. Without rolling papers or a proper way to light it, we improvised. We tore coarse, ash-brown paper towels and rolled them into thick, sausage-like cigarettes.

We lit them eagerly, only to immediately regret it. Flames shot up, and a choking cloud of thick smoke filled the cell. We gagged, coughed, and fanned the air with blankets, doing whatever we could to avoid setting off the alarms. But we were desperate.

We adjusted our method, wetting the paper towels before rolling, making them slightly less combustible. It was still harsh, burning our throats, but it was a fix. A small victory.

Necessity truly is the mother of invention, and I understood that now. Using toothpaste tubes, I crafted a crude pipe. At last, we smoked like gentlemen.

In that moment, we didn't feel like prisoners. We felt like men who had, against all odds, won something back. But the next day, our cells were raided.

The guards stormed in, confiscating our makeshift pipes, our little triumphs of necessity, without hesitation. It was a small loss but a frustrating one.

Soon after, our families managed to send money through our attorneys so we could buy proper cigarettes. A small victory.

Meanwhile, in another cell, an inmate who had also received the dry tobacco bellowed his frustration, demanding rolling papers.

The same guard who had handed us the tobacco chuckled, replying, "Why don't you be smart like those Palestinians and invent yourself a pipe?"

We exchanged glances, suppressing smirks. Even in their attempt to diminish us, they had unknowingly acknowledged our resilience.

CHAPTER SEVEN

THE UNEXPECTED REPORTER
A Voice in the Darkness

That night, as Ayman and I lay in our bunks, caught between exhaustion and wakefulness, a voice suddenly broke the silence.

"Hey, Palestinians, are you awake?"

Ayman stirred. "Yes, we are. Who's this?"

"Terrell." He paused. "Hey, dude, they're talking about you on the radio."

We bolted upright, every nerve electrified. "What are they saying?" I asked urgently.

"Your lawyers say you're not guilty," Terrell replied casually, as if he hadn't just shattered the silence that had imprisoned us.

I leaned against the cold steel cell door. "What else are they saying?"

I pressed, desperate for more.

Terrell sighed, clearly annoyed. "I don't fucking know, dude."

Realizing my impatience, I softened. "Sorry, man. We're just dying to know what's happening."

A pause, then he said with unexpected empathy, "I get it. I'll keep listening and let you know."

Relief flooded my chest. "Thanks, Terrell," Ayman and I replied in unison.

Though he didn't have all the answers, he gave us something invaluable, proof that we hadn't been erased. Beyond these walls, people were fighting for us. Our voices hadn't been completely silenced.

That night, sleep didn't come, but for the first time in days, it wasn't because of fear. It was because of hope.

Over time, Terrell became more than a voice in the dark; he became a lifeline.

His updates came with urgency, sometimes whispered through vents, other times smuggled on scraps of paper. Each message grew more detailed, as though he took it upon himself to be our unseen guardian, ensuring we were never truly alone.

We learned more about him. Terrell, a Black inmate serving life for attempting to kill his cellmate, was feared by the guards and respected by the other inmates.

No one dared share a cell with him. He moved easily through the prison's underground networks, wielding an influence we couldn't fully explain.

He was both feared and revered. But to us, he was someone who, despite everything, chose to look beyond the walls and offer us what we needed most, a connection to the outside world.

One morning, the Black guard who had slipped us tobacco appeared at the food slot. His gaze was softer than usual.

"Who's married to the Kenyan lady?" he asked. Ayman and I exchanged a glance.

"Khader," Ayman replied cautiously. "He's in the next cell."

The guard nodded. "Get ready. It's shower time." Then he disappeared.

A knock came at our door shortly after, signaling our turn. Hesitant, we stepped out, the weight of days without washing finally overpowering any fear. We needed this, needed to feel human again.

Two guards arrived with unreadable expressions. "Hands out," one ordered. We obeyed, extending our wrists through the narrow opening.

The cuffs snapped on tightly. The heavy door groaned open, and we stepped out, cold air hitting us like a slap.

Thick metal shackles encircled our ankles, their weight deliberate. A leather bag filled with sand was fastened to one leg, making each step a laborious shuffle.

The handcuffs were linked to waist chains, which in turn connected to ankle restraints, reducing movement to a humiliating shuffle. It was a parade of power, a ritual of degradation.

The journey to the showers was slow. The guards led us down the dimly lit corridor, their boots echoing off the concrete.

We were nothing to them, just bodies in chains, reduced to a spectacle of forced obedience. At the entrance, the guards unfastened our chains, and we stepped inside. The steel-barred door clanked shut behind us, sealing us into yet another cage.

Through the small gap in the bars, we extended our hands for the final part of the ritual. The handcuffs came off, and for the first time in days, we were unchained outside our cells.

A guard tossed us towels and soap. "You've got thirty minutes," he said flatly before leaving.

For a moment, we stood still. It wasn't freedom, but it was a reprieve, a fleeting pause from the weight of confinement.

Hesitant, we undressed and chose shower heads on opposite sides of the room. The water sputtered, then rushed down, warm and steady. It wasn't just about washing away the grime; it was about reclaiming something deeper, something they couldn't take from us.

Ayman's humming carried me elsewhere, weaving through the steam like a thread pulling me home. I closed my eyes, letting the water wash over me, drifting for a moment.

I could almost hear my friends calling my name, hear the chatter of neighbors, smell the fresh bread, olive oil, and my grandmother's roses in Birzeit.

The song faded, and reality crashed in. We turned to the water not just to cleanse, but to wash away the humiliation, the despair. At that moment, the shower was defiant. It was survival. They could chain our bodies, but not our spirits.

Later, we learned our legal team would visit, more than just Brian, Tony, and Gary. It meant reinforcements. It meant we weren't alone.

A surge of optimism swept through us. Finally, we might get some answers. The suffocating uncertainty of our imprisonment, the endless cycle of racist taunts, had worn us down. But now, there was hope.

For the first time in days, we cracked jokes, even about the guards' racist remarks, transforming their cruelty into fuel for our resilience. Our spirits lifted, no longer weighed down by the terror of worst-case scenarios.

Knowing our families and community were fighting for us felt like fresh air after drowning. We were no longer just prisoners. We were men with voices and people behind us. The balance of power had shifted, if only slightly.

The fear that had gripped us was loosening, replaced by something stronger, anticipation, determination, hope.

Shackled as always, we were led down a dimly lit corridor, the sound of chains echoing with each step. At the end stood a heavy wooden door with a small, grimy glass window.

As we approached, my heart pounded. A face appeared behind the glass, familiar and growing larger. Suddenly, the door swung open, and Brian Hudson stormed in.

His presence was a burst of energy, defiance in a place designed to drain hope. He flashed a quick smile at me before turning to the guards, his expression turning hard.

"What's with the chains?" he demanded, voice sharp with fury. "Get these off now. The media will hear about this brutality!"

His words shot through the room, leaving no room for argument.

"Brian," I called out, louder than I'd intended, the relief clear in my voice. "It's good to see you." He turned back, and his smile softened, his eyes warming with familiarity, humanity.

"Are you guys all right?" he asked gently. "Let's sit down. Leni will be here soon." He shot a cutting glance at the guards. "I'll deal with the chains later."

I studied him, light brown hair, pale complexion, wiry frame. Had he changed? Or had I? One week in this place had felt like a lifetime. But there he was, unchanged, unwavering. As always, a cigarette was tucked behind his ear, a signature move.

Brian wasted no time. He dove straight into the updates, urgency in his voice.

Attorney Brian Hudson in a press conference

The government was determined to deny us bail, portraying us as a flight risk, insisting we stay imprisoned indefinitely. But Brian, ever the fighter, reassured us the battle wasn't over. Our legal team was relentless.

The community was rallying behind us, people offering homes as collateral for our release, a Committee for Justice had been formed, and top legal minds had joined our cause.

"Stay strong," he urged, his voice full of conviction. "These bureaucratic games take time, but we'll win this."

As if summoned by his words, the door opened again, and in walked Leni Weinglass. I had never met him, but I knew who he was, a legend in justice, the man who had defended the Chicago Seven. Now, he stood before us, ready to fight.

We learned that another towering figure, former U.S. Attorney General Ramsey Clark, had also joined the legal team defending us.

Michel Shehadeh with former U.S. Attorney General and member of the L.A. Eight legal defense team, Ramsey Clark

The weight of it hit me all at once. This wasn't just about us anymore. It was bigger. The government had tried to erase us, bury us in a cell, make us disappear. But they had miscalculated. They had ignited something far greater.

We were no longer just prisoners; we were a movement. And we were not alone. Our arrest had been a direct consequence of our pro-Palestinian activism, but the truth was more staggering than we had imagined.

Leni began to unravel the enormity of our situation. "This case," he said, scanning our faces, "is bigger than the eight of you. Much bigger."

A shiver ran down my spine.

"This isn't just about you. This is an attack on the First Amendment. The federal government isn't just coming after activists; they're coming after ideas, associations, and speech. They want to set a dangerous precedent. If they succeed, this won't stop with the Palestinians. It won't stop with immigrants. It won't stop at all."

His words landed like stones in my chest.

"They don't want Americans to know what's happening in Palestine," Leni continued. "The military occupation, the violence, the dispossession, they want to keep it all in the dark. Because if Americans understood, they wouldn't support U.S. policy there."

His eyes locked on ours. "That's why it's you." He paused, letting the weight settle. "But it could have been anyone."

His words landed like a punch. This wasn't paranoia. This was calculated.

"This isn't an isolated case," Leni said sharply. "This is part of something much bigger. A secret strategy, meticulously executed at the highest levels of government."

A cold silence settled over us. We had thought we were fighting for justice. But now we saw the true scale of the threat, an orchestrated effort involving the Vice President, the Attorney General, the FBI, and the CIA.

Institutions we had only seen in the news were now tangled in our lives, treating us, students, young men with dreams, as pawns in a game we didn't even know we were playing.

It felt surreal, like a dystopian novel. A web of power so vast, so meticulously woven, that resistance seemed futile. But we had no choice but to resist.

When Leni and the other attorneys left, we were left in the silence of our confinement, drowning in more questions than answers. What had we stepped into? How far would they go to destroy us?

The late, renowned L.A. Eight attorney Leonard Weinglass

In our cramped cell, Ayman and I sat in silence, lost in our thoughts. We needed to talk to the others. Desperation turned us resourceful.

Using the narrow pipe under the sink, we reached out to Khader and Aiad, trying to piece together fragments of understanding.

The next day, during our brief one-hour reprieve in the

basketball courts, we reconvened. Under the indifferent California sky, we exchanged hurried whispers, passing along scraps of information and theories.

Ayman and I, positioned in the middle court, became the messengers, bridging gaps, relaying fears, and translating the weight of Leni's revelation.

We dissected every word, scouring them for meaning, but no matter how we pieced it together, the picture remained baffling.

But one thing was certain: we were no longer just defendants. We were proof of something far more sinister, a chilling message from a government that had decided to wield fear as its weapon.

We found ourselves trapped in a conspiracy fit for a Hollywood thriller. But this was no script. It was real.

How could we, mere students, be caught in secret government agendas? It defied logic, yet here we were.

But reality, no matter how grim, was the only antidote to despair. We refused to be paralyzed by shock.

The weight of what was at stake, immigrant rights, free speech, and pro-Palestinian activism, pressed down on us. The future of the Arab American community, the right to dissent, hung in the balance.

Fear threatened to consume us, but we couldn't afford it. Too many people believed in us, fought for us. We owed it to them and to ourselves not to crumble.

This wasn't just about us; it was about the right to exist without persecution. About resisting the anti-Arab hysteria that threatened to drown us.

We were Palestinians, heirs to a century of defiance against injustice. Resistance was in our blood.

This was our small piece of that struggle, and we would meet it with unshakable resolve. From that moment, we became sharper, more focused, more deliberate.

When we weren't dissecting legal strategies, Ayman and I would sing Palestinian folk songs, our voices rising through the cold walls.

The melodies wove a fragile thread of joy through the bleakness, a reminder that even here, in this place meant to break us, we were still unbroken.

I devoured books from the inmates' library, finding solace in the written word. Each week, a cart of books made its rounds, and I'd trade the old for something new.

One day, Aiad asked for a recommendation. I suggested *Papillon*, the gripping tale of Henri Charrière's escape from Devil's Island. He later told me it was the first English novel he had ever read, and he loved it.

Meanwhile, Terrell, our neighbor across the hall, kept us updated. The media circus outside raged on, painting us as villains in a spectacle of fearmongering. The day after our arrest, *The Los Angeles Herald Examiner* screamed: "War on Terrorism Hits LA."

The public cheered as the government paraded us as "dangerous terrorists." But through it all, we clung to hope. Not the naïve hope of innocence, but the fierce, unrelenting hope of those who refuse to be broken. We had no choice but to endure, resist, and survive.

Finally, I was able to call my wife. Hearing her voice brought a wave of relief and longing. She recounted the chaos and fear following my arrest, the uncertainty of what came next, and what she and our son, Ibrahim, had been doing to navigate it.

"There's a lot happening," she said. The attorneys were working tirelessly, arranging family visits. The thought of seeing them again, of hearing their voices, was something to cling to in the cold, indifferent walls of prison.

I hadn't held my wife and son in what felt like a lifetime. Maxine and Ibrahim were my only family here, my anchors in a world that had become unrecognizable. But more than anything, I worried for Ibrahim. At three, he was too young to understand the cruelty of what had happened, yet not too young to be haunted by it.

Years later, Ibrahim would tell me about the recurring nightmare that haunted him. In it, he waited for me to return from work, watching the headlights approach from a distance. He would wave frantically, crying out, "Baba! Baba!" But the car would pass him by, and he'd chase it, his small legs moving as fast as they could, his cries fading into the night.

When I asked if he remembered the arrest, he hesitated, "I don't know, Baba. I've heard so many accounts from so many people. Reality blurs with memory."

Despite the uncertainty, the nightmares were real. Fragments of trauma buried deep, surfacing in his subconscious.

The day before the visit, I could hardly contain myself. Maxine, Maria, and Ibrahim were coming, and the anticipation coursed through me. I counted the hours, minutes, and seconds.

The government had scheduled visits for only two of us at a time, a calculated effort to divide us, to stifle any collective strength. It wasn't random; it was a strategy to fragment, demoralize, and erode the will of prisoners piece by piece. A method perfected over time.

We mocked their paranoia, joking about a daring escape, but beneath the humor, we understood the depth of their control.

Still, we'd endure any humiliation, any restriction, for the chance to see our loved ones. Those moments, brief as they were, would be our lifeline. Later, we would pass that strength between us, whispered through the pipe under the sink, exchanged during our fleeting outdoor breaks in the basketball courts.

CHAPTER EIGHT

A COURT OF ANOTHER KIND

Morning arrived with its usual brutality, crude awakening, and a pitiful excuse for a meal. But today was different. This was the day we had been waiting for.

The guards came, shackling us in chains that clanked against the cold floors as they led us through the prison. Each step felt heavier, anticipation pressing against my ribs. The walk to the visitation area seemed endless.

We crossed an outdoor metal bridge-like corridor, attached to the second story of an adjacent building, looming above the prison yard below. From here, I saw the open yard, hemmed in by four identical prison buildings.

The design was efficient, movement choreographed, space optimized, every inch accounted for. The system was a well-oiled machine, ensuring compliance with minimal resistance.

And yet, as I walked, another thought gnawed at me: the same government that had perfected efficiency here was engaged in an exercise of staggering waste. Millions spent, decades of bureaucracy, and untold resources used to prosecute us, eight immigrants who had done nothing more than advocate for Palestinian rights.

The irony was almost unbearable, efficiency in prison design, but wastefulness in political persecution. A government mastering control, yet abandoning reason in the face of paranoia.

Below, inmates moved under the warmth of the Southern California sun, even in January. Most were men of color, living proof

49

of America's warped justice system, where race often determined fate.

Some greeted us from afar, their voices rising in a distant camaraderie. Others were indifferent, caught in their routines. Some had imposing, muscular builds, their bodies inked with tattoos; others were lean, unmarked by ink but marked nonetheless by the system that had ensnared them.

For all their differences, they were unified in soaking up the golden rays of the sun, claiming whatever warmth the world outside their walls offered.

A silent understanding passed between us. For once, the government's paranoia worked in our favor. Isolated from the general population, we were grateful for the distance.

The corridor led to the meeting space. As we entered, I took in the stark, impersonal room, plastic tables and chairs, cheap and familiar, contrasting with the heavy weight of the moment.

Two doors framed the room: the one we entered through and another with large glass panels revealing a sliver of the world beyond these walls.

Armed guards loomed at every entrance, stationed like statues of intimidation. Their presence was suffocating and ridiculous. We, dangerous Palestinian "terrorists", had earned their paranoia.

Then, suddenly, they were there, Maxine, Maria, and Ibrahim, his small hands clasped in theirs, walking toward me. My heart surged. Ibrahim looked older, his face etched with a seriousness no three-year-old should bear. It was as if he understood the gravity of it all.

Maxine appeared thinner, worn down by stress and uncertainty. I fought against the flood of emotions rising within me, willing myself to stay composed.

Then, as Ibrahim crossed the threshold, he turned to the guards and kicked their legs with all his might.

"Let my Daddy go! Let my Daddy go!" Ibrahim shouted, his tiny fists clenched in defiance.

I froze, stunned by his courage. This small child, barely past toddlerhood, stood his ground, his voice ringing out in fearless resistance. The moment should have shattered me, but instead, it filled me with indescribable pride.

I called his name, my voice thick with emotion. He turned, a bright grin spreading across his face, and in an instant, he was in my arms.

Maxine and Maria, with three-year-old Ibrahim on their way to their first visit to Terminal Island to see the L.A. Eight

The outside world, the guards, the walls, the chains, disappeared. There was only him. His warmth, his love, his unshaken belief that I was his, and he was mine.

We sat down, eager to make the most of every second. Maxine quickly filled me in. She and Ibrahim were staying with friends, navigating the chaos. She had lost her job but drew strength from the outpouring of support.

The media storm was relentless. She had stepped forward, giving interviews, making our voices heard.

She told me about the Committee for Justice (CFJ), a growing movement that had taken up our cause. It wasn't just about us anymore; it was bigger. The case had ignited something, uniting people from different backgrounds in a shared fight for justice.

We had lost so much, but in that moment, as I held my son, I realized we had also gained something, a fight worth waging, a truth worth defending, and a love that no prison walls could contain.

The Arab American community rallied behind us, unwavering in their support. They donated, volunteered, and marched, standing shoulder to shoulder with non-Arab allies. Their voices rang out, refusing to be silenced.

For me, Ayman, and Amjad, students at California State University Long Beach (CSULB), the outpouring of solidarity from our fellow students was especially moving.

On campus, they held signs demanding justice: "Free Our Students," "Free Palestinian Political Prisoners." Their chants echoed through university corridors, spilled onto downtown Los Angeles streets, and reached Terminal Island, where they gathered to demand our release.

Students across the country joined in. They understood this wasn't just about us. It was about them, about the right to think freely, to speak without fear, to resist oppression.

The CSULB Daily 49er and The Union covered our case relentlessly, refusing to let our story fade. Every issue brought updates, protests, the legal battle, and the growing movement.

One article highlighted Amar Babu, a CSULB student who launched a hunger strike just days after our arrest. "This is a bold, self-sacrificing effort to demand their release," he declared. His courage electrified the movement.

The visit from Maxine and Ibrahim had been a balm to our spirits, a lifeline that renewed our strength.

When we walked out of that visitation room, we carried something the guards could never chain down, an unshakable resolve. We would fight. We would resist. We would not be broken.

Our bond hearing was set for February 17, 1987.

The charges were absurd, stitched together from the McCarran-Walter Immigration and Nationality Act of 1952, a Cold War relic designed to silence dissent.

They didn't accuse us of personally advocating radical doctrines but claimed we had distributed literature that did. That was enough to justify our imprisonment.

The organization in question was the Popular Front for the Liberation of Palestine (PFLP), the second-largest faction of the Palestine Liberation Organization (PLO).

The specific publications cited were Democratic Palestine and its Arabic counterpart, Alhadaf (The Target). We hadn't written or edited these magazines, but it didn't matter.

The truth was clear: this wasn't about the law. It was about suppression, criminalizing our identity, and making an example of us.

But we refused to cower. This wasn't just our fight; it was a fight for every immigrant, every activist, every person who dared to speak truth to power. To be Palestinian is to be political.

Our history and existence have been politicized since 1917, when the British promised our homeland to the Zionist movement, a land they didn't own, a people they didn't consult.

Since then, politics has been the rhythm of our survival. We devour news, analyze events, and engage in endless debates.

At the time of our arrest, the PLO had nine distinct factions, each regularly publishing newspapers, magazines, pamphlets, and books. These weren't clandestine; they were openly available to Palestinians and non-Palestinians alike. They documented our history, poetry, and aspirations.

Every Palestinian has strong political views. There's a joke: "If two Palestinians meet, they'll have three opinions."

We are, and always have been, news addicts. Whether in refugee camps, Gaza, California, or academia, we follow every development, dissect every headline. Today, social media has replaced magazines and radio, but the obsession remains.

Being Palestinian means living under a microscope, our existence debated, our rights denied, every action scrutinized.

Yet, despite it all, we read, write, and resist. History has taught us one truth, silence is never an option.

We track everything, resisting Israeli occupation, daily life in Palestine, who died, who married, and even the latest gossip.

We don't just follow events at home; we live them, breathe them, carry them in our bones. Every shift, every moment of defiance, every injustice inflicted on us ripples through us, no matter how far we are from the land.

If you see two Palestinians arguing, at a wedding, a funeral, or a restaurant, it's politics. Always politics.

Even my eighty-three-year-old mother-in-law in Ramallah doesn't start a phone call with "How are you?" She begins with the latest report from Palestine, including who was arrested, what the occupation forces did today, and the latest news. For us, politics isn't just a discussion; it's survival. It shapes our fate and our homeland's future.

For me, it's proof that I exist. No matter what they try to erase, I am still here.

Because of our connection to politics, the breadth of the McCarran-Walter Act was staggering. It wasn't just a tool to target activists; it was a weapon against thought itself.

Under this act, any Palestinian, or any immigrant, who so much as reads a Palestinian magazine or picks up a book critical of U.S. foreign policy could be labeled a threat. These publications were available in university libraries, ethnic bookstores, and cafés. Professors taught from them, journalists cited them, and they were part of public discourse.

Simply reading, gifting, or recommending them made you a target. Ideas were dangerous. Thinking was dangerous. Knowledge itself was a crime.

The government's shockwaves didn't stop there.

On February 10, just one week before our bond hearing, they struck again.

This time, their target was Julie Mungai, Khader's wife, a

Kenyan national with no criminal record or political history, with no reason to be caught in the government's crosshairs.

Michel Shehadeh, Amjad Obeid, Khader Hamideh, and Julie Mungai, with lead attorney Marc Van Der Hout, alongside members of the Committee for Justice

Her initial charge? A minor visa violation, typically resulting in a fine or bureaucratic hassle. But suddenly, the government escalated her case, slapping her with ideological charges under the McCarran-Walter Act, the same law used against us.

The punishment was swift. Julie was thrown into solitary confinement at Sybil Brand Prison for women. She wasn't a threat or criminal, but the government saw her as guilty by association. Her confinement had nothing to do with national security; it was political theater, a deliberate act to intimidate and silence us.

They wanted to send a message: resist, and this is what happens.

Years later, Sybil Brand was shut down, officially due to poor conditions and damage from the 1994 Northridge earthquake. Poetic justice, perhaps.

On February 15, just two days before our bond hearing, repression widened again. Bashar Amer, a Palestinian student, was arrested during a chemistry exam at Chaffey College. Like Julie, he was charged with visa violations and, like us, accused under the McCarran-Walter Act. The L.A. 7 became the L.A. 8.

The L.A. Eight, with their spouses, alongside attorneys Paul Hoffman and Marc Van Der Hout

The government's efforts to suppress us intensified, but our resolve remained unbroken. They could add more names, build higher walls, but they would never silence us.

As non-U.S. citizens, the government exploited a loophole to press charges. If we had been citizens, the First Amendment would have protected our rights to free speech and association, no matter how unpopular our ideas.

The Reagan administration and those who followed wanted to deny immigrants these rights, creating a system where dissent was criminalized for some and protected for others.

For over three years, the FBI had been watching us, tracking our movements, recording our conversations. They planted an agent in the apartment next to Khader and Julie's for months, observing through a hole in the wall. They infiltrated our lives with informants, installed hidden cameras, and attended our events. At one point, they even used surveillance satellites.

Despite all their efforts, their millions of dollars spent, and their surveillance, the FBI found nothing, no criminal activity, no illegal acts.

The truth was revealed in April 1987 during a Senate Intelligence Committee hearing. Former FBI Director William Webster, under oath, admitted: "The individuals who were arrested in California had not been found to have engaged themselves in terrorist activities."

He added, "If these individuals had been United States citizens, there would not have been a basis for their arrest."

The admission was damning. They hadn't arrested us for any crime; they had arrested us because they could. With no evidence of federal violations, the FBI handed the case to the INS, rebranding it as an immigration matter.

FBI spokesperson Susan Shnitzer attempted to justify it, claiming that while no federal violations were found, they thought turning over information to the INS would be "helpful." This politicized the INS, transforming it into a weapon against political activists.

But Webster's testimony exposed the truth. To mitigate the damage, the INS dropped ideological charges against six of us, downgrading the charges to minor visa violations. However, for Khader and me, the political charges remained. Over the years, the government continued to manipulate the law, reshaping it to sustain their persecution.

The government failed to prove us criminals, so they tried another method: making us disappear. The political charges against Khader and me kept shifting, with the laws reinterpreted to fit their agenda.

We were students, visible members of the community. How could a responsible government make such baseless accusations against us, people who lived openly?

In our cell, we tried to pass the time, remain calm, and cling to normalcy. Terrell's updates became lifelines. "Your lawyers are good. They defend you good." "Radio says the government can't prove shit." His simple words reminded us that the world outside was watching, that we weren't alone.

When it was time for our usual shower routine, something felt different. We had adapted to detention's strange rhythms. This time, we knew there were no surprises. But halfway to the showers, the guards took us to the prison barbershop, a tiny room crowded with barbers, helpers, and an absurd number of guards. The system here wasn't about efficiency; it was about control.

We sat in cheap wooden chairs, each assigned a barber. I got a trim, while Ayman went for a bold change. "No one's seeing me anyway, might as well take the chance for a zero haircut," he joked. Today, he's bald.

Afterward, we enjoyed our shower time. The warm water wasn't just cleansing, it was healing. For thirty minutes, we weren't prisoners; we were just men feeling human again.

Later that afternoon, I was reading a book, and Ayman was lost in thought, when a knock came at the door. The same Black guard who had inquired about Julie was there. "Get ready," he said,

"You're going somewhere."

Confused, we followed him down a quiet hallway, without the usual chains or weights. He was polite, even smiling. At the end of the corridor, he opened a plain wooden door and motioned us inside. The room was nearly empty, with a few cheap metal chairs scattered around and a dusty TV mounted on the wall.

The guard unlocked our handcuffs, turned on the TV, and casually announced, "The Lakers game is about to start." We stared, stunned.

For weeks, we had been treated as high-risk prisoners, shackled and isolated. But now, we were sitting in an unlocked room with a guard, watching basketball?

The absurdity of it all was overwhelming. Later, Khader explained that during a conversation about Julie, he had mentioned his love for basketball. The guard, a die-hard Lakers fan, had taken it upon himself to make sure we didn't miss Game 6 of the NBA Finals between the Los Angeles Lakers and the Boston Celtics.

This wasn't an official prison privilege. It wasn't part of any policy. It was one guard, seeing us as people, not enemies. A small, defiant act of kindness in a place designed to strip kindness away.

As the game began, I, never much of a basketball fan, found myself swept up in the energy.

We laughed, cheered, groaned at missed shots, shouted at the screen, and exchanged high-fives, not just with each other, but with the guard. We were all Lakers fans, prisoners and guards alike, united in our devotion. Whenever Magic Johnson or James Worthy delivered a perfect pass or made an impossible shot, the room erupted.

When Larry Bird or Kevin McHale answered back for the Celtics, we groaned, but the frustration dissolved into exchanged glances, silent reassurances that our team would come back swinging.

But Kareem Abdul-Jabbar was different. We loved him, not just for his skyhook or dominance, but because he was one of us. A pioneer. He took an Arabic name, embraced Islam, and stood for something bigger than basketball. Like Muhammad Ali, Kareem gave us pride, a counterweight to the relentless Arab-bashing and Islamophobia we faced daily.

Then came the triumph. The Los Angeles Lakers defeated the Boston Celtics 106-93, winning the championship (4-2) and cementing their dominance in the greatest rivalry in basketball. A game for the history books. And for the L.A. 8, it was a game we would always remember.

For two hours, everything shifted. The prison walls, the chains, the interrogations, all of it faded. We weren't prisoners, and the guard wasn't our jailer. We were just men watching a game. A victory not of politics, but of humanity.

That night, for the first time since our arrest, we slept peacefully. The smallest gestures can ease immense pain. But this wasn't just kindness; it was a sign.

For years, the U.S. government spun a web of fear, portraying Palestinians as bloodthirsty extremists. We, the L.A. 8, were the latest players in this propaganda campaign, a manufactured threat to justify repression.

But inside these walls, the narrative was falling apart. If a guard, raised on anti-Palestinian rhetoric, could sit with us, joke with us, and celebrate a Lakers win, how real was the illusion?

That crack in their narrative emboldened us. We weren't just fighting for our freedom anymore; we were fighting for the truth. And that was what the government feared most.

From the start, their plan had been clear: indefinite imprisonment. No bail, no trial, no real evidence, just "secret evidence." Something we couldn't see or challenge. But their illusion was breaking. And we were still standing. Now, everything hinged on February 17.

The upcoming hearing wasn't just a legal proceeding; it was a fight for our existence. If we won, we walked out on bail. If we lost, we stayed behind bars. For how long, no one knew. The weight of it pressed down on us. This would be a fight like no other.

CHAPTER NINE

THE BOND HEARING
Inside the Theatre of Repression

February 17, 1987, the day of reckoning, had arrived. The stakes couldn't have been higher. This hearing would determine our fate: bail or indefinite imprisonment, buried under so-called "secret evidence."

The courtroom felt less like justice and more like a battlefield. Both sides had come prepared for war.

On one side, the U.S. government, a modern-day Goliath, arrayed agents and prosecutors from the FBI, CIA, INS, State Department, and local law enforcement. They had the weight of empire behind them, a machine designed to crush dissent, set examples, and silence voices like ours before they could gain traction.

Their attorneys were seasoned, ruthless professionals, armed with unlimited resources and political backing. They had money, influence, and power to shape the law to their narrative.

And then there was us. We had no vast legal team, no deep pockets, no institutional clout. Immigrants, students, workers, ordinary people swept into a storm far bigger than ourselves. But we were not alone.

Volunteer attorneys stood with us, fighters for justice driven by principle, not profit. Our case relied on community donations, activist support, and the outrage of those refusing to let injustice go unchallenged.

Where the government had intimidation, we had courage. Where they had repression, we had the Constitution. Where they wielded fear, we held truth.

It was David versus Goliath, not just a legal battle, but a defining moment in America's civil rights history. The outcome wouldn't just affect us; it would set a precedent for immigrants, activists, and anyone who dared speak truth to power. History was watching.

The vans arrived in the dark parking lot beneath the Federal Building, headlights slicing through cold emptiness. Under heavy guard, we entered a groaning elevator. The only sounds were rattling shackles and humming fluorescent lights. When the doors opened, a long, sterile corridor stretched ahead.

Armed guards lined it at regular intervals, hands on weapons, eyes scanning for threats that didn't exist. The 30-pound black bands around our ankles forced slow, awkward shuffles, prisoners from a bygone era. The scene was grim, theatrical, surreal.

At the corridor's end stood our friends and families behind a metal barrier, faces tense, eyes wide with anticipation. Reporters passed through metal detectors, while five armed guards flanked the courtroom entrance, amplifying the spectacle. This was staging, not security.

The government wanted our supporters to see us chained, subdued, stripped of dignity. They wanted fear broadcast: "dangerous terrorists," obedient, powerless.

Inside, the rules were rigid and calculated, designed to strip humanity. Families were banned. Only the respondents, eight attorneys, and four reporters would be allowed. No familiar faces. No comfort.

Cameras lingered in the corridor, capturing every clinking chain, every forced expression. The message was clear: Look at them. Be afraid.

But then something unexpected happened. The moment our supporters saw us, the silence was shattered.

A wave of emotion surged through the corridor, cheers, greetings, shouts of encouragement, and hands flashing the victory sign. We raised our shackled hands in response, mirroring their energy, feeding off their strength. In that instant, the power shifted. The government's psychological warfare had failed.

They wanted despair, fear, broken families weeping quietly. Instead, the cameras captured triumph, defiance, and unbreakable solidarity. The corridor crackled with energy, a moment of resistance instead of submission.

Everything about our case had been meticulously choreographed, including chains, camera angles, and security measures. It was a photo op of repression: heavily shackled men, paraded under extreme security, presented as the nation's most dangerous criminals. The design worked. Few questioned it. Few asked why such precautions were needed for people who had committed no crime.

The public consumed the images passively, their perception shaped by sound bites stripped of context and a media trained to validate state narratives rather than challenge them. Noam Chomsky had a term for this: Manufacturing Consent.

"If we don't believe in freedom of expression for people we despise, we don't believe in it at all."

"The smart way to keep people passive and obedient is to strictly limit the spectrum of acceptable opinion, but allow very lively debate within that spectrum."

Our case was a textbook example. The Palestinian cause had to be kept outside that spectrum. Any notion that Palestinians might have a legitimate grievance or just cause was dangerous. We were reduced to caricatures, a perfectly engineered spectacle to create fear, justify repression, and reinforce the idea that Arab Palestinian immigrants were permanent suspects. A Hollywood stereotype brought to life.

When I later saw the footage, it struck me: we looked exactly like the Hollywood version of "terrorists." Young, disheveled Arab men, unshaven, brown-skinned under harsh courtroom lights. And to complete the picture, a Black Kenyan woman was included.

Michel Shehadeh and the late professor Edward Said, and his widow, at a community event

This wasn't a coincidence. It was calculated. For decades, mainstream media and pop culture had conditioned the American public to associate these images with terror, violence, and evil: the dark-skinned enemy, the fanatic, the faceless villain. A script Americans were trained to recognize without question.

Professor Edward Said, in Orientalism, exposed how the "East" was portrayed as "anti-American, hypocritical, manipulative, untrustworthy, rude, barbaric, religious, traditional, rough, and dirty" (Said, 1978). This wasn't mere cultural bias; it was a political tool, weaponized with precision. In a country where image is the trial and perception matters more than facts, fear becomes political currency. Guilt is decided long before the hearing begins.

While we sat inside the Federal Building awaiting our fate, another scene unfolded outside. Lenora Tong, writing for the Long Beach Union, captured it vividly:

"February 17, 1987, was a day to remember for all of us who attended the Vigil for Justice."

Students, professors, and community members had gathered on the steps of the Federal Building, standing together in defiance of our arrest and looming deportation.

Their signs were bold: "Free Our Students" and "Free the Palestinian Political Prisoners," cutting through the tense air. Among them was Amar Babu, the CSULB student on a hunger strike since Thursday, a visceral act of solidarity.

Not everyone in the crowd supported us. A Zionist heckler paced the steps, shouting, "Deport them now!" and "Hell, No, PLO!" For a fleeting moment, energy flared, with some firing back, "Long Live the PLO!" But the moment passed quickly. Yet when the media reported, that brief exchange became the story, overshadowing the hundreds of peaceful demonstrators.

Tong's account continued: for the next half hour, nervous anticipation filled the air. People paced, smoked, and whispered hurriedly. "What's going on?" "Have you heard any news yet?" Some, unable to bear the waiting, took the elevator up and down, desperate for any sign of progress.

Inside the Federal Building, we waited too. Each of us was assigned our own lawyer; group defense wasn't allowed. My attorney was Paul Hoffman, from the ACLU and Amnesty International, a calm, personable man in his late forties. His thinning white hair framed a fair, medium-built frame, and his clear, steady voice cut through the noise, instilling confidence. He was more than a lawyer; he was an anchor.

The rest of our team was equally formidable. Renowned legal minds like Lenny Weinglass and Mark Rosenbaum stood with us, not just attorneys, but believers in justice, fighters who saw this case as a moral battle as much as a legal one. Over time, we built mutual respect, camaraderie, and a shared mission. In that courtroom, defending us meant defending justice itself.

Word arrived that the Jordanian Consul had come to observe. On paper, we were Jordanian citizens, carrying Jordanian passports, a bureaucratic consequence of history and occupation. But our identity was never in question. We were Palestinians.

We refused his attendance, making it clear: if deported, it would be to Palestine, not Jordan. This was more than bureaucratic; it was a stand against erasure. Israel had long attempted to erase Palestine from geography, history, and memory, declaring Jordan the "alternative homeland." This fabrication had been rejected by most Palestinians as a lie, a justification for ethnic cleansing.

There was an immediate danger, too. Deportation to Jordan meant prison and suppression for our activism. The Jordanian government feared political activism, especially Palestinian activism, and punished dissent. In private, we joked at the irony: if the U.S. insisted on deporting us to Palestine, Israel would be forced to acknowledge our right of return, a bureaucratic technicality turned historic victory. The consul left disappointed, but the matter was political, not personal.

Finally, the hearing began. We took our places on the pews reserved for the accused, ankle weights strapped on, facing the judge's elevated bench. The courtroom was packed, reporters ready, sketch artists capturing every detail, the tension, the expressions, the weight of the moment.

Judge Roy Daniels opened the proceedings with calculated neutrality. The hearing, he stated, had one purpose.

Would we be granted bail or held indefinitely? Judge Daniels emphasized that his decision rested on two questions: whether we were flight risks or threats to the public.

Fitzsimmons, the government attorney, began by accusing us of affiliation with the Popular Front for the Liberation of Palestine (PFLP).

"The PFLP advocates illegal methods to overthrow the U.S. government and other so-called imperialist governments," she declared. "It is responsible for terrorist activities resulting in deaths worldwide. The respondents belong to this organization."

Lenny Weinglass, commanding in his dark gray suit and red tie, led the defense. Every movement deliberate, every word precise, his booming voice demanded attention.

"The government has no evidence, and they have none," he said. "This is posturing, a sham designed to make flamboyant allegations in hopes the media will carry them."

Mark Rosenbaum followed. "The respondents are not being prosecuted for actions," he argued. "They are being prosecuted for ideas."

None of us had written or edited the publications cited as "evidence." None of us had committed any crime. We categorically denied PFLP membership. Yet we were on trial.

Paul Hoffman widened the scope. "This prosecution has a chilling effect on free speech, especially within Arab American and immigrant communities."

Each attorney dismantled the government's case piece by piece. No criminal acts. No violence. Only ideas, associations, and political beliefs were on trial.

Then Fitzsimmons made her move, requesting a private discussion with the judge, citing "national security concerns." She claimed U.S. Attorney General Edwin Meese III had personally ordered her to present "secret evidence", so sensitive that neither our attorneys nor we could see it.

Judge Daniels was incredulous. "You're offering witnesses claiming these people want to overthrow the U.S. government, and you haven't put this in writing?"

Fitzsimmons admitted there were no written statements. Meese had ordered the FBI agent to testify only to the judge, in chambers.

This was no longer just about our case; it was about setting a dangerous precedent, normalizing undisclosed evidence in deportation cases, and stripping defendants of the right to defend themselves.

Judge Daniels' face hardened. "If you have anything against these people, you should be able to say it in front of the public and media."

Fitzsimmons' confident voice dropped to a near whisper. "I can't tell you. I've been ordered to do it this way by the Attorney General of the United States."

The courtroom held its breath. "Tell me what you can," the

judge demanded, patience worn thin.

"You're asking me to deny them bail on the basis of evidence no one is allowed to see?" Fitzsimmons stammered, her face flushed, searching for words that didn't exist.

Reporters gasped, pens flying across notepads. For all the government's power, resources, and theatrics, they had produced nothing, no proof, no justification, no case. Judge Daniels exhaled sharply; his patience finally spent.

"From what you've told me, I'm not persuaded they are a bail risk."

For the first time, the government's case, its secrecy, fear-mongering, and manufactured hysteria, began to collapse. Judge Daniels had made his stance clear: no secret evidence, no backroom deals, no hidden testimony.

Yet Melanie Fitzsimons refused to back down. She pleaded for two government witnesses to testify in a private "in-camera" session, away from public scrutiny.

One was an FBI agent who "couldn't testify in open court due to national security concerns." The other was a female witness, whose life, Fitzsimons claimed, would be "endangered" if she appeared publicly.

Judge Daniels wasn't having it. "You should have been prepared with an affidavit from government agencies attesting that revealing such testimony posed a national security risk," he said firmly.

Fitzsimons had nothing. Her desperation was palpable. Running out of arguments, running out of time, she even whispered, "Can I at least approach the bench and whisper it in your ear?"

The courtroom froze. Daniels blinked, bewildered, glanced

around, then down at his papers. A ripple of laughter spread through the room, mocking whispers, incredulous glances. Had she really just asked to whisper "evidence" into a judge's ear?

Daniels straightened, voice sharp: "If you have anything against them, present it in the open. Tell me what you can, anything."

Desperate, Fitzsimons pivoted, attempting to invoke fear, branding the PFLP as an "international Marxist/Leninist terrorist organization" bent on overthrowing the U.S. and Israel.

She threw out every fear-inducing buzzword: "Marxist. Leninist. Terrorist. Overthrow. PFLP." But the attempt fell flat. Daniels didn't flinch.

"This is a bad group, I'll give that to you," he said. "Now, what do you have on this gentleman?"

Each defendant faced the same impasse. Daniels demanded evidence in open court. Fitzsimons repeated, "I cannot tell you."

Hours passed. The government had failed to provide evidence, justify their claims, or explain why we should be denied bail.

Cornered, Fitzsimons made one last attempt. She offered a "private look" at a 45-page classified FBI report, the supposed foundation of the government's case. Daniels, clearly fed up, refused.

"I am going to ask you to do that in public," he snapped.

Fitzsimons stood frozen, mortified. Cornered, defeated, her attempt to wield the name of Attorney General Edwin Meese backfired spectacularly. Instead of bending, Daniels stood firm.

She was trapped, between the unyielding judge and the superior demanding she argue the indefensible. For a fleeting moment, I almost felt sorry for her.

Judge Daniels sighed, rubbing his temples, voice edged with disappointment. "It bothers me that the government isn't telling the court why these respondents are a flight risk and should be denied bail."

The frustration was palpable. The government had every opportunity to present evidence, yet their case stood empty.

The tiny, packed courtroom vibrated with tension. Then, finally, Judge Daniels straightened, shuffled his papers, and spoke with finality:

"I'm not convinced by the government's argument. Here is my decision."

The room stilled. No one breathed.

"I am ordering that the respondents be released on their own recognizance. Three on bonds: Bashar Hussam Amer, $3,000. Naim Nadim Sharif, $2,000. Aiad Khaled Barakat, $500."

The judge exited. For a moment, no one moved. Then Lenny Weinglass turned to us, triumphant. "You're free," he said. "You're all free." The room erupted.

For Fitzsimons, it was a spectacular unraveling. For us, it was vindication.

This wasn't just a legal victory; it was a resounding affirmation of everything we had fought for: justice, constitutional rights, the very idea that immigrants, Arabs, and dissenters had the right to exist, speak, and resist.

It belonged not just to us, but to every person who had marched, donated, protested, and believed.

We jumped, laughed, embraced, our attorneys, supporters, and anyone within reach. High-fives flew. The energy was electric, unstoppable. Even the media sketch artists put down their pencils and clapped. The consensus was unanimous: the government had lost, and justice had won.

A surge of happiness overtook me, so powerful, so pure, words could not capture it. Except for the births of my children and grandchildren, I cannot recall a moment so all-consuming. Tears welled in my eyes, and I saw others around me overcome by the magnitude of the moment.

This wasn't just our victory; it belonged to all of us. Yet freedom was not immediate. The guards arrived, chains in hand. Our hands were shackled again as we were escorted back to Terminal Island for one last night, waiting to be processed for release.

Officially, we were still prisoners, but we knew the truth. The government had suffered a crushing defeat. This was a victory not just for us, but for justice itself.

Outside, a different celebration unfolded. Three hundred students, activists, professors, and families had gathered, a movement united in resistance.

Lenora Tong of the CSULB Union captured the moment:

"The tension finally broke when a man ran to the top of the steps, shouting that three of the detainees had been released."

The crowd erupted. Cheers, hollers, clapping, whistling, the weight of weeks of fear and anxiety lifted instantly. Palestinians linked arms, forming a circle.

And then, in downtown Los Angeles, on the very steps where injustice had been contested, they danced the Dabkeh. Their feet pounded the pavement, voices rising in unison:

"Lah Lah Lah ou Lah Lah! El-Houriyin El-Wahda Kermala!"

A Palestinian national song of freedom. Tears and laughter mingled.

For that moment, the crowd became one body, one voice, an unstoppable force.

The anticipation grew. Where were we? Would we walk out into the arms of those waiting?

Groups gathered at every exit, hoping. But the news disappointed, processing meant we would spend one more night in prison.

Lenora Tong of the CSULB Union reported:

"Soon, the anticipation of seeing the former detainees mounted as groups crowded around the exits where they might possibly be released. The waiting crowd diminished by 6:00 PM upon news that they [defendants] were being released at Terminal Island."

Our release would take another day to complete. Julie Mungai, Khader's wife, however, was freed immediately from Sybil Brand Women's Prison.

Lenora captured the crowd's disappointment at not seeing us, but also the joy of Julie's release:

"We did get to see Julie, the Kenyan woman, as she emerged gracefully from behind the metal fences."

Julie stepped out, graceful, unbroken, a Black African woman branded a threat, persecuted for association, now walking free.

Then another victory. Lenora wrote:

"Amar finally ended his five-day water-only fast when we persuaded him to eat sushi with us in Little Tokyo."

His protest had begun in sorrow and resistance; it ended in celebration, solidarity, and triumph.

"This day will not be forgotten for a long time to come," Lenora wrote.
"It represents a civil rights victory for all people. It motivates us to continue the fight for full civil rights and due process of law for everyone."

Though I hadn't been there, her words transported me; I could see the faces, hear the chants, feel the relief.

This was our first legal victory against the government. The fight for justice, dignity, and full civil rights was far from over. But on that day, we had momentum, and we would carry it forward, no matter how long the road ahead.

The rational choice would have been to let it go, to accept the court's decision. But the government was not rational. Their overzealousness overpowered logic; their stubbornness eclipsed restraint.

It was brawn, not reason, that drove their decision to continue this prosecution by any means.

We were Palestinian immigrants. Nobodies, in their eyes. Yet we had done the unthinkable, stood up to the U.S. government and won.

It was a sore defeat for them, and they were not finished. Outside the courtroom, Fitzsimons faced reporters, sharp and clipped:

"I am extremely disappointed with the judge's decision to allow dangerous people to go free."

She refused further comment, but her bitterness was clear. We were free, but only for now. The U.S. government was not done with us.

CHAPTER TEN

ALIEN TERRORISTS AND UNDESIRABLES:
A Contingency Plan

Less than two weeks after our arrest, on February 7, 1987, The Los Angeles Times dropped a bombshell.

Investigative journalist Ronald Soble had uncovered a leaked report exposing a terrifying government plan.

Soble was no ordinary reporter, a two-time Gerald Loeb Award winner and co-recipient of the National News Emmy for Outstanding Coverage of a Continuing Story. He pursued every lead, every document, every whisper of wrongdoing. His reporting was essential reading, not just for journalists, but for us.

As a journalism student, I studied his work closely, treating it as a masterclass in investigative reporting. His ability to peel back layers of secrecy, expose hidden truths, and turn complex legal battles into gripping narratives fascinated me. I read not just to stay informed, but to learn.

Soble's reports revealed the full scope of the government's intentions: a secret contingency plan targeting "alien terrorists" and "undesirables." The 42-page document, titled Alien Terrorists and Undesirables: A Contingency Plan, outlined a shadow legal framework designed to bypass the Constitution, strip due process, and justify mass apprehension, detention, and deportation.

Under the guise of "protecting national security," the U.S. government had prepared a system to erase civil liberties in a single stroke. What had begun as a case against eight individuals was now part of something far larger, far darker. This wasn't just about us; it was about every immigrant, every activist, every person who challenged power.

Soble's reporting tore away the illusion that our case was merely legal. It confirmed what we had long suspected, we were pawns in a broader government scheme. His work validated our fight, revealing the scale of manipulation and the coordinated efforts of multiple agencies.

Through his investigation, Soble exposed contradictions, a lack of evidence, and internal inconsistencies within the government. Most explosively, he revealed the classified contingency plan. Our attorneys obtained a copy, likely leaked by a whistleblower, and we, the defendants, the Committee for Justice, legal experts, and allies, studied it meticulously. Every line, every word, was analyzed.

No one defended it. Even the government tried to downplay its significance. Reading it myself was surreal. Had I not lived through it, I might have doubted its existence. This wasn't a theory; it was a meticulously crafted blueprint for mass repression.

The plan had been devised by the Alien Border Control Committee (ABC), an interagency group formed in June 1986 at the recommendation of then-Vice President George H.W. Bush's Task Force on Terrorism.

The ABC was no minor bureaucratic initiative. It comprised representatives from the most powerful agencies in the country: INS, FBI, CIA, U.S. Marshals, U.S. Customs, the State Department, and the Executive Office for Immigration Review.

At the helm was INS Commissioner Alan Nelson, overseeing four working groups, each executing a specific part of the plan. One of these groups, Group Three, had objectives that mirrored the charges brought against us:

"Expulsion from the United States of alien activists who are not in conformity with their visa status."

"Expeditious deportation of aliens engaged in support of terrorism while protecting classified information and its sources." (INS Office of Intelligence, October 1, 1986)

The connection was undeniable. Six of us were accused of visa violations. Two, as permanent residents, were accused of "supporting terrorism." All of us were Palestinian activists. This wasn't about law; it was political repression, a campaign to silence, criminalize, and expel pro-Palestinian voices.

The plan extended far beyond us. It outlined methods for the INS to deport nationals from seven Arab countries and Iran, even specifying a "target group" of 10,000 individuals from Algeria, Libya, Tunisia, Iran, Jordan, Syria, Morocco, and Lebanon. These were students, workers, and community members, ordinary people marked for existence alone.

Our arrests weren't justice. They were a test run. If the government could use secret evidence, mass deportation, and political persecution against us, the system could be applied to thousands. We weren't just fighting for our freedom; we were exposing a framework that could destroy countless lives. Thanks to Ronald Soble's reporting, the world began to see the truth.

The scale of the contingency plan was staggering. It wasn't a guideline; it was a blueprint for national repression. Massive resources would be deployed to target, detain, and deport nationals from seven Arab countries and Iran, using the McCarran-Walter Act as the legal weapon.

The Act instructed federal agencies to "routinely hold any alien so charged without bond," as they had tried with us, ensuring indefinite imprisonment. Personnel from the INS, FBI, U.S.

Customs, and CIA were to execute the operation. This was not an immigration crackdown; it was a political purge.

Most chillingly, the plan included mass incarceration. A 1,000-acre federal facility in Piney Woods, near Oakdale, Louisiana, was designated for thousands of Arab American detainees. It would feature high-security fencing, surveillance, sanitation infrastructure, and a modern internment camp.

The parallels to World War II's Japanese American internment were stark. Over 125,000 Japanese Americans had been forcibly detained under Executive Order 9066; now, Arab Americans were targeted under the guise of "national security."

Adding bitter irony, the mayor of Oakdale at the time, George Mowad, was of Lebanese descent, a town about to house America's next mass incarceration project.

The plan's legal strategy meticulously sought to circumvent constitutional protections, leaving detainees with no recourse or way out.

Key tactics included "Registry and processing procedures," modeled after the 1979 Iranian student registry, but focused on individuals flagged by the CIA, FBI, and other agencies as "alien undesirables" or "suspected terrorists."

The plan leveraged anti-Communism provisions in the McCarran-Walter Act to bring political charges, just as they had done with us, and supplemented them with technical immigration violations, like overstayed visas, to ensure fallback charges if the main accusations failed.

Closed hearings shielded proceedings from public scrutiny under the pretext of "national security," while secret evidence could be presented "in camera" to immigration judges, guaranteeing a legal process stacked in the government's favor.

Every one of these methods had been deployed against us, the L.A. 8. Every move mirrored the plan's tactics, as if our trial had been a test run for a far more dangerous agenda. This was not just about us; it was about reshaping civil liberties in the U.S.

The leaked contingency plan outlined a blueprint for institutionalized discrimination, targeting Arab and "Middle Eastern" communities for surveillance, detention, and deportation. For us, it confirmed what we had long suspected: we weren't just targets; we were symbols. The message was clear, challenge the government's narrative, resist, and this is what awaits you.

Despite our legal victory, the system was relentless. It had not finished with us. Meanwhile, the mayor of Oakdale, Louisiana, expressed delight in his town's selection for Arab American incarceration, citing the "economic benefits", revealing indifference to the human rights crisis unfolding under his watch.

At the time, part of the Oakdale Correctional Center was already holding "Marielitos," Cuban refugees from 1980. By November 1987, nearly 1,000 detainees, furious over a new U.S.-Cuba agreement, took hostages and set fire to the prison. Chaos erupted. The facility built for Arab Americans was now the site of a violent rebellion, but the government did not dismantle it. Instead, it was perfecting the system for future populations.

Historical Parallels

The year 1987 was pivotal. While the U.S. refined its plans for mass detention, the First Palestinian Intifada erupted in December, the "Rocks Intifada", a three-year uprising against Israeli occupation led by ordinary Palestinians armed with stones, defiance, and unbreakable will. It became a global symbol of Palestinian resistance.

As Palestinians rose in the Occupied Territories, the U.S. government enacted its own crackdown at home, targeting Arabs and Muslims. The contingency plan was explicit: in the event of a domestic terrorist emergency, the INS's mission was to "Locate, apprehend, and remove a body of aliens from the U.S."

The INS, once a routine immigration agency, was being repurposed as a tool of political repression. Registration, surveillance, mass deportation, the echoes of history were deafening.

For Palestinians in the West Bank and Gaza, the occupation meant daily humiliation, home demolitions, arrests, and killings. For Palestinians and Arabs in America, the "Contingency Plan" meant surveillance, detention, and deportation. Two different battles, unfolding in parallel. But the enemy was the same.

The mechanisms of repression, whether in Nablus or in a Los Angeles courtroom, were part of the same war against resistance. We had won a battle in court, but the broader fight for justice, dignity, and the right to exist and resist was far from over.

The plan had deep roots, tied to escalating hostility between the U.S. and Libya under Reagan. In August 1981, American jets shot down two Libyan planes over the Gulf of Sidra. Reagan celebrated it as a "demonstration of U.S. power against enemies of freedom." Four months into his presidency, he closed the Libyan embassy, branding Qaddafi's government a sponsor of terrorism.

Following the Gulf of Sidra incident, the Reagan administration spread fear of Libyan "hit squads" allegedly entering the U.S. to assassinate officials. There was no evidence, no confirmed threats, but fear alone justified action. To "preempt" the imagined danger, the U.S. launched a registration program for Libyan immigrants. It was the first step in a broader strategy targeting all Arab Americans.

Tensions escalated further in April 1986, when U.S. airstrikes on

Libya, retaliation for the Berlin nightclub bombing, killed three Libyans, including Qaddafi's adopted daughter, and injured 229. The strikes pushed U.S.-Libyan relations to the brink and intensified domestic scrutiny of Arab Americans. Preventive measures followed: expanded registration, surveillance, and preparation for mass detention and deportation.

The pattern was clear: fear first, registration next, then repression. What began with Libyans in 1981 was now targeting all Arab Americans. We weren't just witnessing history; we were living it.

The Plan's Legal Hurdle

The legal hurdle was significant. In 1979, during the Iranian Revolution, attempts to register Iranian Americans failed because no law justified targeting an entire ethnic community. The Contingency Plan proposed a workaround: find a precedent, push it through the courts, and reshape legal interpretations to justify mass surveillance and deportation.

The government's goal was clear: use a ruling to justify mass registration, surveillance, and deportation. The case they chose? Ours. The L.A. 8 case wasn't simply about deporting eight Palestinian and Arab activists. It was about establishing a legal precedent to target Arab Americans nationwide. We weren't just defendants, we were the battleground.

If they won, the legal foundation for a broader crackdown would be set. Our arrests weren't about visa violations or political associations; they were about creating a justification for a larger, insidious operation. We were test subjects.

The Contingency Plan was more than theoretical; it was a playbook, and our case was its first trial. It outlined a step-by-step strategy for mass targeting, executed precisely in our prosecution: weaponizing the McCarran-Walter Act with political charges, adding technical immigration violations as fallbacks; holding closed hearings under the guise of "national security"; presenting secret evidence to the judge while denying access to our attorneys and us; attempting to detain us indefinitely.

Our attorneys dismantled their script in court, proving we were never an isolated case. We were the experiment, the sacrificial scapegoats, the eight Palestinian and Arab activists and one Kenyan spouse, chosen to build a foundation for mass repression.

The irony was brutal. While the government painted Arab Americans as a terrorist threat, it ignored actual acts of terrorism against the community. On October 11, 1985, the Santa Ana office of the American-Arab Anti-Discrimination Committee (ADC) was bombed. Alex Odeh, the ADC's regional director, a Palestinian American activist, poet, and civil rights leader, was killed.

The FBI identified the attackers as members of the Jewish Defense League (JDL), a far-right extremist group founded by Rabbi Meir Kahane, infamous for calling to violently expel Arabs. The JDL had been designated a terrorist organization. Yet Alex Odeh's murder remained unsolved, no arrests, no prosecutions, no justice.

While the government used "national security" to criminalize us, real terrorist attacks on Arab Americans were ignored or downplayed. The message was clear: Arab Americans could be labeled "terrorists" for their political beliefs, but when Arab Americans were victims, their lives were disposable. The L.A. 8 case was not about national security; it was political suppression.

Alex Odeh's murder was symptomatic of a broader system that criminalized Arab voices and treated Arab lives as expendable. Years later, as Western Regional Director of the ADC, his legacy, unresolved murder, and the injustices he endured became deeply personal. I wasn't just continuing his work; I was carrying his fight forward. Justice, however, doesn't stop at one battle; it follows you, shaping how you endure captivity, reclaim your voice, and define freedom, even after release.

CHAPTER ELEVEN

REST TONIGHT, FIGHT TOMORROW
The War Didn't End, We Just Got a Head Start

At last, we were processed out of Terminal Island Federal Prison. But freedom, as it turned out, carried its own weight.

One of the most unexpected goodbyes was to Terrell, our self-styled "radio reporter" and neighbor across the corridor. Hardened by the prison system yet surprisingly sympathetic, Terrell had become an unlikely link to the world outside.

His whispered updates, casual remarks, and streetwise analysis gave us something invaluable, a sense of time moving forward. Why did he do it? Was it a quiet rebellion against the system? A way to break the monotony of his own sentence? Or simple solidarity?

We never asked. But his presence mattered. And as we parted ways, there was an unspoken understanding: even behind bars, solidarity finds a way to survive.

As we gathered our meager belongings, it struck me how little remained of the lives we had before our arrest. Watches, hands frozen at the moment we were torn from our world. Cigarettes, currency, comfort, and control. The last balance in our inmate accounts, a rigid $20 limit, rationed dignity, managed by our families.

That number was more than a rule; it was a reminder: you own nothing here. Not even your right to survive.

Then, for the first time in what felt like forever, we were free. No chains. No cells. No guards guarding us, only guards guiding us.

We stepped onto the bridge-like corridor overlooking the recreation yard, the final threshold between captivity and the world beyond these walls. Below, inmates moved through their routines, walking in circles, lifting weights, playing basketball, and smoking. Life went on, indifferent to our departure.

It felt surreal. After all the months, the hearings, the humiliations, we were simply walking out. Just like that.

I inhaled deeply, filling my lungs with air that no longer smelled of antiseptic soap and steel. Freedom had a scent of its own. For the first time in months, I let myself believe this wasn't just a pause in the nightmare, it was the beginning of the end.

Below, prisoners turned their faces upward, recognizing the look of men being freed. Some waved. Then came a familiar call," Cigarettes! Cigarettes!" A prisoner grinned, gesturing for us to toss some down. We exchanged a glance, smiled, and without hesitation, threw down the last of our cigarettes.

A scramble erupted below, laughter, shouting, quick deals struck on who got what. It was a small act, but for me, it was a full circle.

On my first day in the San Diego jail, I had found a half-smoked cigarette left behind by someone unknown, and in that moment, it had meant everything. Now we had done the same. A gesture of defiance. A gesture of solidarity. A moment of shared humanity.

As we walked toward freedom, I carried a simple truth: even in the darkest places, resistance survives in the smallest of acts.

Outside the prison gates, members of our political defense team from the Committee for Justice (CFJ) were waiting, the heroes who had fought, organized, and refused to give up.

The air felt different. For weeks, our world had been corridors and concrete. Now we stepped into something else, open, uncertain, and alive. And then, the swarm descended.

Media cameras flashed as reporters surged forward, shouting questions, hungry for a soundbite. One caught up to me just as I reached the car.

"What was the best part of all of this?" she asked eagerly.

"Getting out," I replied without hesitation, slipping into the car before she could ask more.

Even in freedom, I felt a strange sense of displacement. The blue sky, the warmth of the sun, the sheer openness of space, it all felt surreal.

Inside, our guide from the Committee for Justice tried to ease the tension with light conversation. I appreciated the effort, but my mind was elsewhere. I was free, but unsettled. Outside, yet unsure of what awaited.

Our guide, Carol Wallace, was assigned to Ayman and me. Her presence was warm, genuine, and joyful. She didn't treat us like clients or political figures, just people. She told us we were headed to a reception at the Beverly Hills Law Building, hosted by CFJ, a gathering of supporters, attorneys, and families. A moment to celebrate, a small victory, however uncertain the future.

The Beverly Hills Law Building was more than a venue. Built in 1947 by architect Rowland Henry Crawford, it stood as a Southern California gem, its red-brick façade trimmed in white, a walkway framed by neat greenery, elegant yet unpretentious.

The Beverly Law Building in Los Angeles

It was a strange contrast, from steel cages to this quiet refinement. The eight of us gathered outside, waiting to enter as one. Julie joined us, freshly released from Sybil Brand Institute for Women, the day before. Even in freedom, our transport had mirrored our pairings in captivity, as if the bonds forged behind bars were meant to last.

We stepped forward together. The grand wooden doors opened, and attorney Gary Silbiger stood waiting, his face glowing with pride and relief.

Then came the sound, applause, cheers, and our names being called. Over a hundred supporters filled the hall, their faces lit with joy, defiance, and solidarity.

For the first time since our arrests, we weren't fighting; we were home.

The reception hall exuded old-world elegance, chandeliers hanging from high ceilings, polished wood panels, and shelves lined with legal tomes. A long conference table had been transformed into a banquet of victory, covered in food and drinks arranged with care.

As we entered, the applause swelled, echoing off the walls. The sound hit like a wave, overwhelming, uncontainable, real. Their joy wasn't just for our release; it was a shared triumph. We had fought. We had won. And for that moment, it was all worth it.

For the first time in three weeks, we felt not just freedom of movement, but freedom of spirit. The energy in the room crackled like a live wire, a pulse of triumph coursing through the crowd. Eyes shone with pride, hands clapped in unrestrained celebration, each applause a thunderclap of defiance and relief.

Faces glowed with exhilaration, reflecting the collective power of resistance and solidarity. This wasn't just about us; it was about justice winning, however briefly.

The reception captured what had made our victory possible: organizing, community, and relentless resistance. At its heart was the Committee for Justice (CFJ), founded by Brian Hudson and Tony Hall with one goal, to get us out.

They had coordinated our legal defense, mobilized the media, and, with Glennis and Linda Lotz from the American Friends Service Committee (AFSC), exposed the government's secret "Alien Terrorists and Undesirables" plan.

This night wasn't just a celebration of our freedom; it was a reaffirmation of the battle ahead. A fight for civil liberties. Against anti-Arab racism. For government transparency and accountability.

Because this wasn't over. This was only the first victory in a war far from won. It wasn't just a party; it was a collective triumph. Everyone in that room had played a part in our freedom.

The applause wasn't just for us; it was for them. For every person who had marched, organized, donated, and fought. And so, we clapped back in gratitude, a shared moment of recognition, solidarity reflected in every smiling face.

Still, as I stood there amid the celebration, something tugged at me. We were wearing the same wrinkled, slightly dirty clothes we'd been arrested in three weeks earlier. For a moment, I felt self-conscious, until I looked around and realized no one cared.

Not about our clothes. Not about the grime of captivity. Not about the exhaustion in our eyes. They saw us for what we were: not former detainees, but symbols of resistance. Surrounded by warmth, admiration, and unwavering solidarity, I had never felt more at home.

The room pulsed with life, familiar faces, our legal team, community leaders, activists, and supporters. Yet one presence mattered most: my wife and my son, Ibrahim, the little boy whose televised plea, "I want my Daddy back!" had touched hearts across the nation.

Now here he was, the youngest person in the room and the undeniable star. Everyone doted on him, showering him with affection. This was his victory too.

The catered food looked delicious, platters of finger foods, drinks flowing, the air thick with laughter and relief. But I couldn't eat. The whirlwind of emotion, the press of people, the sheer intensity of it all left me drained. I was happy, deeply happy, but utterly exhausted.

More than anything, I wanted to hold my family, to step away, to breathe. To process. But tonight wasn't about retreat. It was about honoring those who had fought for us, who had refused to give up. Their victory was our victory.

So, I embraced it, smiling through the exhaustion, exchanging knowing glances with my fellow detainees. They felt it too. We had survived. Together. And that solidarity, the same force that had sustained us in detention, was carrying us now through this moment of triumph.

Three weeks had felt like an eternity: the isolation, the racist taunts, the endless uncertainty about our fate. Every day had been about survival. Now, surrounded by freedom, bright lights, and cheering faces, the noise felt almost disorienting.

I longed for quiet, for a moment alone with my wife and son, away from cameras and conversation. Then guilt crept in. These people, our friends, our community, our defenders, had given everything. They had marched in the cold, faced hostility, and stood unwavering when it would've been easier to turn away. I owed them this moment.

So, I pushed aside the fatigue and the yearning for solitude. I shook hands, hugged familiar faces, and let their joy wash over me. I let myself be present. Because this wasn't just a homecoming, it was a victory. Tonight, we weren't just detainees released from custody. We were living proof that resistance could prevail.

As the night stretched on, the energy began to ebb. One by one, people hugged us, congratulated us again, and began to leave. They had given everything to this fight, and now they were going home, readying themselves for the battles still ahead.

A few of us remained, our attorneys, our closest allies. Then Brian Hudson, head of the Committee for Justice steering committee, called for a meeting. He introduced Dan Stormer, our lead attorney. Dan stood before us, voice steady, words deliberate.

"The deportation hearing is set for April."

Dan's tone carried the weight of a general preparing his troops for battle. "We need to be meticulous in our preparation."

Then, with an encouraging smile, he added, "Now go home. Get some rest. Congratulations to all. This was an important win, but there's still a lot of work ahead."

He was right. This was a battle won, but the war was far from over. For the government, this had ceased to be a mere legal case. It had become a mission, a crusade fueled by career ambitions, political pressure, and the desperate need to justify years of wasted resources. A career-defining fight. And they weren't going to back down.

Neither were we. Their overzealousness would keep the fight alive for years. But so would our defiance.

That night, we found refuge in the home of Khalid El Borno, a dear friend who opened his Northridge house to us without hesitation. It wasn't just a place to sleep; it became our temporary headquarters, a space to regroup, reflect, and plan.

The eight of us, along with our families, filled the house, transforming it into something between a home, a war room, and a sanctuary.

As I lay in Khalid's home, exhaustion finally settling into my bones, I reflected on the enormity of the journey ahead. The joy of the day lingered, tempered by the reality of what was still to come. And yet, for the first time in weeks, I felt hope.

A night's sleep not on a prison bunk. A night with my wife and son beside me. A night without the clang of steel doors. It was a balm for the spirit, a quiet renewal of resilience.

Soon, we were drawn back into the fight, immersed in the legal and political battles still unfolding. Rumors began to circulate, whispers that our case had reached the global stage.

That Soviet Premier Mikhail Gorbachev had mentioned our case to President Reagan during their December 1987 summit in Washington, D.C.

That he had criticized the United States for its hypocrisy on human rights, using our case as an example.

Was it true? We didn't know. But the fact that it was even plausible spoke volumes about how far the ripples of our struggle had spread. The world was watching.

Media and Public Opinion Shift

As time passed, the media narrative began to shift. At first, reporting was cautious, detached, almost clinical. But soon, the tone hardened. Journalists and editorial boards began openly calling on the government to end its persecution of us.

- "Arab Groups See INS Bias" – Washington Post, 2/7/1987
- "Is This Case for Real?" – Los Angeles Times Editorial, 2/10/1987
- "Yearning to Breathe Free" – by Anthony Lewis, New York Times Editorial, 2/13/1987
- "Free Speech Rights" – San Francisco Chronicle Editorial, 2/19/1987
- "Combating Terror or Persecuting Unpopular Views?" – by Stephen Chapman, Chicago Tribune Editorial, 2/25/1987
- "Arab Bashing at the INS" – Detroit News Editorial, 3/27/1987

These were only a few of the growing number of reports and opinion pieces that exposed the government's overreach. They revealed the absence of evidence, condemned the excessive force used against us, and warned of the chilling effect this case could have on civil liberties.

What had begun as a deportation case was now understood for what it truly was, a test of the nation's conscience.

A fight against government overreach.

A warning sign for the erosion of fundamental freedoms.

The Cartoon That Said It All

Perhaps nothing captured the essence of our case more vividly than a now-famous illustration by Los Angeles Times cartoonist Paul Conrad.

The image was stark, rendered in bold black and white, its high-contrast design demanding attention.

At the top, the word "Amerika" appeared in large, capitalized letters, white against a black background, slightly tilted, creating an atmosphere of unease. The spelling, with a "k," was a deliberate and politically charged choice, invoking echoes of authoritarianism, repression, and state control.

Beneath the title, a row of shadowed silhouettes marched across the frame, identical figures, hunched forward, heads bowed, ankles bound by chains. They moved in unison, their rigid, synchronized steps evoking a sense of mechanical submission, as if stripped of humanity.

The top half of the background was jagged, cut by harsh, short black lines that gave the image a sense of confinement and claustrophobia, contrasting with the burdened figures below.

At the bottom, a small caption read simply:

"Arab immigrants jailed in Los Angeles. News item."

That understated line grounded the piece in reality. The entire illustration felt like a protest-era political cartoon, raw, direct, and unflinching. It was a scathing critique of U.S. policy, exposing the hypocrisy of a nation that prided itself on liberty while chaining those who dared to dissent.

It became a symbol, not just of our case, but of a country confronting its own reflection. A visual indictment of creeping authoritarianism. A warning disguised as art.

Over the years, the media attention surrounding our case grew immense. I compiled three thick volumes of newspaper clippings, articles, editorials, interviews, and several VHS tapes containing televised coverage. The L.A. 8 case had become a landmark in civil rights discourse.

In time, it would be remembered as the longest deportation case in U.S. history, and one of the most significant civil rights battles of the 1980s. But more than that, it endures.

The echoes of our struggle still reverberate, not only in courtrooms and classrooms, but in the streets, in protests, in every demand for justice made by those deemed "undesirable."

Today, our case is studied in law schools across the country as a defining moment at the intersection of immigration law, civil liberties, and government overreach. But it is more than just precedent.

It is a warning.

A reminder of what happens when fear governs law, when repression replaces freedom, and of what happens when ordinary people refuse to be silenced.

Thirty-eight years later, in 2025, under President Trump's second administration, history is not merely rhyming; it is repeating itself.

The arrest of Mahmoud Khalil, a Palestinian student activist at Columbia University, for his pro-Palestinian speech, stands as a chilling echo of McCarthyism's dark legacy. It is as if that era never truly ended, only paused, waiting for the right moment to reawaken.

Once, the McCarran-Walter Act was used to silence and deport political dissidents, weaponizing immigration law against free speech, first in the 1950s, and then in the 1980s, with our own case, The L.A. 8.

We fought to strike down its unconstitutional provisions, and we succeeded.

Yet today, it feels as if those same forces were never defeated, only dormant, reborn under new names, new laws, and new justifications: the PATRIOT Act, or whatever comes next.

The targeting of Mahmoud Khalil, the renewed surveillance of immigrants, and the widening assault on free speech expose a sobering truth, the struggle is far from over.

We once believed we had buried these tactics in history. But they linger still, old ghosts wearing new uniforms, the machinery of repression humming beneath the surface, waiting for the next excuse to turn its gears.

And yet, just as before, resistance rises. Voices refuse to be silenced. And history, once again, warns us in no uncertain terms:

This fight is not over.

CHAPTER TWELVE

RENT, RESCUE, AND RESISTANCE
Ordinary People, Extraordinary Acts in a Time of Crisis

In the months following our release from jail, amid the legal and political chaos of the L.A. 8 case, moments of grace occasionally broke through, small yet profound.

One of the most unexpected came from our Chinese landlords. They didn't know us as headlines or as "the L.A. 8." They knew us simply as neighbors, familiar faces who stopped by their small convenience store, exchanged greetings, and shared the quiet routines of everyday life.

They saw us not as controversy, but as tenants, customers, and people. And as immigrants themselves, they understood the unspoken weight of what we were enduring.

So, without hesitation or fanfare, they waived our rent for a month. A quiet, deeply human act of solidarity, one that needed no words to express its meaning.

Wolfi's Rescue Mission
But perhaps the most surprising act of kindness came from Wolfi.

Wolfi was our neighbors' dog, an older, St. Bernard type with a calm temperament and soulful eyes. My son Ibrahim adored him.

Their friendship was simple and pure, built through small moments in our fenced backyard, where Ibrahim would play, and Wolfi would keep watch, tail thumping gently against the ground.

One afternoon, while I was cooking, Wolfi began to bark. At

first, I ignored him; he wasn't the type to make noise without reason, but I assumed it was nothing.

Then the barking grew louder. Urgent. Persistent. He darted between our back door and the yard, barking, pausing, and barking again, his eyes fixed on me.

Something was wrong.

I stepped outside, and Wolfi immediately bounded toward the fence, stopping to look back as if beckoning me to follow. His bark had changed; it wasn't random or playful. It was deliberate.

And then I saw him.

Ibrahim was stranded on the wire fence, his tiny hands gripping the mesh, his face streaked with fear. He had climbed up for an adventure but couldn't find a way down, and was too afraid to jump.

Wolfi had seen him before I did. When Ibrahim called out for help, it was Wolfi who answered.

I ran to the fence, lifted Ibrahim into my arms, and held him close. When I turned, Wolfi stood quietly now, tail swaying slowly, eyes calm and satisfied, as if to say, "You're welcome."

That moment stayed with me. It changed the way I saw dogs forever.

I had always liked them, but that day, I came to love them. Wolfi hadn't just barked. He had understood. He had intervened. He had cared.

A creature with no words, no motives, no obligation, had shown us the purest form of empathy.

In the darkest times, kindness finds a way, sometimes through a friend, sometimes a stranger, and sometimes through a barking, tail-wagging guardian.

That day with Wolfi deepened not only my love for dogs but also our bond with our Chinese landlords and neighbors, Kit and her husband, though his name, regrettably, escapes me now.

Kit managed both the property and the store, always smiling, always ready to help. Her husband, busy with his day job, was more of a quiet, occasional presence, but both radiated quiet generosity and compassion.

Their simple acts, waiving rent, offering concern, reminded us that solidarity often comes from the most unexpected places.

At that time, our lives were peaceful and full of purpose. Most of us were students, building careers, nurturing dreams.

I was at California State University, Long Beach, majoring in magazine journalism, an irony, considering the government would later accuse me of distributing "undesirable publications."

Amjad was studying engineering. Ayman was training to be an architect. Bashar was studying to become a pharmacist. Khader and Julie had both graduated from the University of Oregon, he in business administration, she in accounting.

Aiad worked in construction, and Naim was employed at a department store. We were students, professionals, hardworking immigrants, ordinary people trying to build ordinary lives. Yet the government twisted our identities into something sinister.

At the time of our arrest, Khader and I were permanent residents, Green Card holders, on the verge of becoming naturalized U.S. citizens. We had already applied for citizenship, Khader, months before me.

Then, through the Freedom of Information Act (FOIA), we obtained an FBI report by Frank Knight, the lead agent in our investigation. His words confirmed our worst suspicions:

"The arrests occurred when they did because Hamide had filed for United States citizenship and was inquiring, through his attorney, why it had not been granted. The INS, by statute, had to either provide him with his citizenship or attempt to deport him."

That was it. It wasn't about national security. It wasn't about terrorism. It was about stopping Khader from becoming a U.S. citizen.

Faced with two options, grant citizenship or fabricate a reason to deport him, the government chose the latter.

To justify their actions, they built a story.

Khader was painted as the "ringleader" of the Popular Front for the Liberation of Palestine (PFLP) on the West Coast. I was labeled his "right-hand man" in charge of Southern California. The others were cast as members of a supposed "PFLP Cadre."

It was pure fabrication, guilt by association, designed to criminalize Palestinian activism and establish a dangerous precedent for political repression.

We monitored every development closely. Volunteers recorded TV news segments while we attended meetings, press conferences, and legal briefings. Every evening, we gathered over dinner, watching the footage, strategizing our next steps.

It was exhausting, but also invigorating. We were not alone.

Khalid's house, our base of operations, buzzed with energy and resistance. It became more than a refuge; it was a living, breathing center of solidarity. Volunteers cooked, cleaned, and handled logistics. We all contributed, balancing the weight of the legal struggle with small acts of normalcy.

Despite the relentless stress, the house felt alive, a place of exhaustion, yes, but also of belonging. It was a hub of community and defiance, where resistance was built one meal, one meeting, one conversation at a time.

We didn't stay still for long. Invitations poured in from Arab American communities across the country. We traveled constantly, speaking at events, explaining our case, raising awareness, and fundraising to keep the legal fight alive.

But not everyone welcomed us with open arms. Reactions within the Arab American community were mixed. Many stood with us, but others were afraid.

When news of the secret "Contingency Plan" spread, it sent shockwaves through the community. Fear became tangible. This was no longer about eight individuals; it was about an entire population at risk.

The idea that Arab Americans could be rounded up and imprisoned in concentration camps was no longer an unthinkable nightmare; it was written policy.

Some chose courage and solidarity. Others withdrew, terrified to even be associated with our names. Fear cast a long shadow.

And yet, amid that fear, acts of bravery and generosity shone all the brighter.

One moment I will never forget happened in Baton Rouge, Louisiana. After a speaking event, I asked the audience for donations to support our legal battle.

A young man, a student working a minimum-wage job at a fast-food restaurant, stood up, walked to the front, and signed over the back of his two-week paycheck.

He didn't hesitate. He simply gave everything he had.

It was likely that he'd have to borrow money just to make it through the month, yet he still chose to give. That gesture left an indelible mark on me.

I may have forgotten his name, but never his courage. To this day, I still wish him every good fortune.

For his selflessness. For his courage. For proving that even in fear, some still found the strength to stand up.

But not everyone could. Not everyone was ready to stand in the spotlight. Many in the Arab American community chose to distance themselves from our case entirely.

And I understood why. Fear is powerful. The threat of being watched, labeled, or losing everything you've built, it's enough to make anyone retreat into silence.

Many of our people had come to the U.S. to escape exactly this. They had fled persecution, political repression, and war. They had left behind countries where speaking out meant prison, exile, or worse. The idea that they could face that same danger here, in America, the land they thought was safe, was terrifying.

This wasn't just politics. It was survival. Protecting their families, their businesses, their futures. I never judged them. I couldn't. I knew the cost of fear.

But I also saw how some responded, not with distance alone, but with erasure. They began to reshape their very identities, hoping invisibility might grant them safety.

Mohammad became Mike. Hanna became John. Abdalla became Al. Faik became Frank. Nasser became Victor. Osama became Sam.

These weren't just new names; they were masks. Silent shields against suspicion.

It wasn't about shame. It was about survival. The instinct to blend in, to pass unnoticed, to slip beneath the radar of a society that now viewed Arab identity as a threat.

I don't say this to criticize, but to reflect on what the government's actions did to our community. The chilling effect was real. The pressure to assimilate, to mute your name, your language, your culture, was immense.

For some, holding onto their identity was a statement of principle. For others, letting go was a matter of protection. Both choices carried pain.

Across the country, Arab American households quietly removed anything that could tie them to their heritage.

Arabic books, magazines, and newspapers, gone. Posters of Palestinian villages, discarded. Flags, heirlooms, and even cultural art were packed away, hidden, or destroyed.

It was an erasure born of fear.

This case didn't just impact eight defendants. It chilled an entire generation. It scarred a community that had only just begun to find its voice.

The Fight Went Beyond Our Community
But we refused to be silenced.

I traveled coast to coast, speaking at universities, churches, synagogues, and civil rights events. I spoke to Democrats,

Republicans, Libertarians, Greens, and anyone who would listen.

We gave interviews to television and radio stations, newspapers and magazines, and later, to podcasts and YouTube channels. I wrote articles for The Los Angeles Times, The New York Times, The San Francisco Chronicle, The Oregonian, and The Washington Report.

I told our story, not just in English, but in Arabic, so that both worlds would know the truth.

Khader was equally active, engaging with diverse communities, while the rest of the L.A. 8 supported as much as their circumstances allowed.

For me, it became a movement without pause, city to city, hall to hall, meeting people from every walk of life: Black, Latino, and Asian communities; Jewish, Christian, and Muslim organizations; labor unions, student groups, civil rights coalitions.

Each carried their own story of struggle, their own scars, their own definition of resistance. And in their solidarity, I found strength.

The Japanese American Community: A Profound Connection
Of all the communities that stood beside us, one left the deepest mark, the Japanese American community.

They understood our fear better than anyone. Because they had lived it.

They knew what it meant to be branded a national security threat. They knew what it felt like to be rounded up, stripped of dignity, and forced into detention camps while the world looked away.

They didn't just empathize, they remembered.

I had the privilege of sharing the stage with survivors of the

Japanese American internment camps, and the bond I felt with them was both profound and humbling.

They didn't just offer words of support; they stood with us, marched with us, and fought beside us.

With members of the Japanese American community and survivors of the Japanese American concentration camps after World War II, following a speaking engagement at the Japanese American Museum

They knew that what had happened to them should never happen to another community again.

During those first few months after our release, our lives revolved entirely around the case. We were still staying at Khalid's house in Northridge when one afternoon, Khader, Amer, a close friend and supporter, and I went out to run errands.

Amer had driven up from San Diego to help us. I was behind the wheel. We stopped at the Wilshire Hyatt Hotel in Los Angeles for a meeting with potential supporters. Nothing seemed unusual.

While we were inside, Amer stepped out to retrieve some

documents from the car. That's when he saw it, a man had opened the trunk and was walking away with a briefcase full of critical legal papers.

Amer immediately confronted him.

The man was calm, well-dressed, clean-shaven, polished shoes. When caught, he didn't run or panic. He simply placed the briefcase on the ground, turned, and walked away without a word.

It was too deliberate to be random.

We reported the incident to the Committee for Justice (CFJ) to document it, and soon, the media picked up the story. But this wasn't an isolated event. There was a pattern.

Two attorney offices were broken into. A car tied to the case was tampered with. Naim's house was burglarized, but nothing valuable was taken. Coincidence? Unlikely.

We had no concrete proof that the government was behind these acts, but the suspicion was impossible to shake.

Our lead attorney, Marc Van Der Hout, told the Los Angeles press, "It's possible the FBI or another government agency was involved," though he added, "There was no evidence to substantiate the claims."

Of course, there wasn't. That was the nature of COINTELPRO-style tactics, untraceable, deniable, buried beneath layers of plausible deniability.

But the message was unmistakable. The timing of our arrests. The intimidation of our lawyers. The strange break-ins and missing files. All of it pointed to one goal,

They wanted us to feel watched. To feel unsafe. To feel hunted.

Living Under the Sword of Damocles

But we couldn't afford to drown in paranoia. The next battle was already upon us. Our deportation hearing was set for April 28.

We met with our lawyers daily, mapping legal strategies, reviewing documents, coordinating with CFJ, and keeping media attention alive.

Even my wife, Maxine, was now part of the fight. She had been hired as CFJ's office manager, turning our family's ordeal into a shared mission.

We were ready. The government had tried everything, arrests, secret evidence, psychological warfare, but we were still standing.

We had faced intimidation and refused to yield. The deportation hearing would be another storm, but this time, we were prepared to face it head-on.

After a month at Khalid's home, we finally returned to our old address. Kit's warm smile and Wolfi's wagging tail greeted us at the door.

It was a small, quiet moment, but it carried immense weight.

For the first time in weeks, something felt familiar. Steady. Normal.

A glimpse of stability in a life that had become defined by uncertainty.

I was determined to reclaim what I could, to finish my journalism degree at California State University, Long Beach, and find a sense of direction despite everything that hung over us.

But it wasn't easy.

Our lives had been turned inside out. We didn't know if we would be allowed to stay or if we'd be deported. And if deported, where would we even go?

We were stateless. Unwanted in the U.S., and with no country willing, or able to take us in.

It felt like living under the sword of Damocles, always waiting for the next blow to fall.

Despite everything, I refused to give in to despair. "Deal with the present," I told myself. "Fix now, and the future will take care of itself." Easier said than done.

But as a family, we made a choice: we would live as best we could. We would face each problem as it came and fight the injustice forced upon us. Would we survive it?

We didn't know. But we had no choice except to try.

Through it all, I clung to my core values: be a good man, walk with justice, and keep your soul free. I believed that if I held on to those principles, everything else would follow.

Still, life had more obstacles in store. Every new day brought another legal twist demanding our attention.

The case felt like an earthquake. The arrests had been the eruption; what followed were the aftershocks, each one exposing new layers of the government's obsession.

One of the first aftershocks came on March 22, 1987, when the FBI released an 81-page report, the product of a three-and-a-half-year investigation into the Arab American community. At the center of it all? Us, the Los Angeles Eight.

The report laid everything bare. The government had infiltrated

Arab American community events. They had surveilled churches, mosques, and cultural centers. They had even spied on us in our homes. Nothing was sacred.

They intercepted our letters. They searched the baggage of travelers connected to us. They photographed people at airports and tracked those who picked up shipments of magazines.

The U.S. Customs Service had even intercepted and copied address books and donor lists from community events.

This wasn't ordinary surveillance. It was a full-scale operation, an obsession with dismantling Arab American activism before it could grow into real political power.

And at the center of it all stood one man: the FBI's self-styled crusader, Frank Knight.

He wasn't just an investigator. He was the architect of our persecution, the face of the Los Angeles Eight prosecution.

This wasn't just a job for him; it was a mission.

Physically, he was unassuming, six-foot-three, with white hair, and glasses. He looked more like a college professor than an FBI agent. In fact, he had been one, a teacher for seven years before joining the Bureau.

But beneath that calm, academic exterior was a relentless determination. He wasn't merely pursuing suspects; he was orchestrating a campaign against an entire community. And we were his chosen targets.

The release of Knight's report confirmed what we already suspected, we had been watched for years. Our community had been infiltrated. Our private lives, our movements, our friendships, all under surveillance.

The government was determined to destroy us. But if they were obsessed with silencing us, we were equally determined to fight back.

Frank Knight was no ordinary agent. A Seattle University graduate, a former regular Army officer who had served in Europe and Vietnam, he had spent nearly two decades in military and intelligence work before joining the FBI.

By the time our case began, he had been stationed in the Los Angeles field office since 1978, specializing in counterterrorism. He was not a passive bureaucrat; he was a man on a mission.

According to his own testimony:
- 1980: Assigned to an FBI squad investigating international terrorism.
- Late 1983: Tasked specifically with monitoring individuals associated with the PFLP.

That meant the FBI had been watching us for over three years before our arrests.

Three years of phone taps, informants, wiretaps, and silent infiltration, all to build a case that still produced no crime.

CHAPTER THIRTEEN

FROM MUNICH TO LOS ANGELES
Manufacturing a Threat

Knight's justification for his investigation? The 1972 Munich Olympics attack carried out by Black September.

That incident became his pretext. With the upcoming 1984 Los Angeles Olympics, federal and local law enforcement launched an enormous security operation, forming the Olympic Task Force to hunt for possible "terrorist threats."

In his report, Knight wrote: "The PFLP is well-known to the FBI as a terrorist group." Because Black September was affiliated with the PLO, Knight conflated them, collapsing complex political distinctions into a single false category.

We were Arab. We were politically active. We supported Palestinian rights. That was enough for him.

The Olympics came and went without a single incident involving us. No crimes planned, no crimes committed, no evidence of any threat. And yet, Knight's investigation didn't stop.

His surveillance didn't stop. His obsession didn't stop.

Why? This was never a search for truth. It was a crusade.

Was it ideology? Racism? Career ambition? Blind loyalty to U.S. anti-Palestinian policy? Perhaps all of the above.

What was clear was that Knight knew we were not terrorists. He admitted as much under oath. Yet he kept pushing for our deportation.

He wanted a victory. A precedent. A message.

Frank Knight was not merely investigating us; he was hunting us.

Frank Knight's Words: A Window into His Mindset
Knight's reports read like scripts from Cold War propaganda, filled with sensational claims, ominous language, and outright fabrications.

A few excerpts:

"They [the Eight] organized fundraisers on behalf of the PFLP, at which money was solicited for the stated purpose of supporting terrorist acts."

"I witnessed from a secreted area; the keynote speaker announced the names of moderate Palestinians who were on the PFLP hit list."

"The event was listed as a dinner dance, but in actuality, it was a PFLP fundraiser, and the money raised in San Bernardino would be going to support the PFLP in Syria and Lebanon."

"The decorations depicted violence through posters of men carrying assault weapons and banners opposing peace negotiations."

"There was nothing about humanitarian interests, just PFLP militant subjects."

Dramatic accusations, but with one glaring flaw: no evidence.

After over three years of surveillance and the full power of the FBI, Knight failed to produce a single shred of proof.

Why? Because the claims were false.

We weren't raising money for terrorism; we were raising funds for Palestinian schools, hospitals, and orphanages.

We weren't targeting "moderate Palestinians"; we were criticizing collaborators with Israeli occupation, a longstanding part of Palestinian political discourse.

The so-called "violent posters" were commemorations of martyrs, young men killed by Israeli forces.

But to Knight, our very existence was threatening. Our Arabic language was "terrorist language." Our Dabkeh dance clothes, "terrorist attire." Our music, "terrorist tunes."

In his eyes, we weren't students, workers, or activists. We were terrorists. Not because of anything we had done, but because of who we were.

Michel Shehadeh and Amjad Obeid, with two other friends, performing Palestinian Dabkeh in front of Los Angeles City Hall. The clothing was labeled "terrorist attire," and the music "Terrorist tunes," by FBI agent Frank Knight

Knight's mission wasn't about truth. It was about feeding a pre-written narrative and satisfying the government's hunger for a Palestinian "terror cell" on U.S. soil.

It was about proving a theory even when no proof existed.

But under the light of the courtroom, his narrative collapsed. The fabrications unraveled. The government's arguments fell apart.

And Frank Knight failed.

Judge Stephen V. Wilson's Cutting Remark

During one court hearing, Federal Judge Stephen V. Wilson perfectly captured the absurdity of the government's case:

"It seems to me that someone who doesn't speak Arabic, infiltrated one of these hafles (parties), and decided that these people were terrorists according to the color of their attire and the tune of their songs."

With one sharp observation, the judge exposed the racism, ignorance, and blind prejudice that had fueled the entire investigation.

Knight's accusations weren't based on facts; they were rooted in fear.

It took ten long years, an entire decade after our ordeal began, before we finally had the chance to depose Frank Knight under oath.

July 1997, Washington, D.C.

Before Robert H. Haines, notary public for the District of Columbia, as part of the Arab American Anti-Discrimination Committee (ADC) vs. Reno case.

For the first time, Frank Knight would have to answer for his words. His fabrications would be tested. His authority stripped bare.

For the first time, he couldn't hide behind his badge, his reports, or the veil of secrecy that had long protected him.

Khader and I were there to witness it.

A Legal Team Ready for Battle

We were not alone. David Cole, our brilliant attorney from the Center for Constitutional Rights, led the charge. His three assistants, Andrew Camelio, Jeff Smagula, and Hannibal G. Kemerer, backed him with precision and focus.

Phyllis Bennis, our trusted private investigator, sat beside us, meticulously noting every inconsistency. And Houeida Saad, general counsel for the ADC, brought her sharp legal acumen and quiet strength.

On the government's side were Michael P. Lindeman, Edward J. Duffy, and Madeline Henley, representing the Department of Justice's Office of Immigration Litigation.

This was no routine cross-examination. It was an interrogation of the very foundation of the government's case.

For four full days, David Cole grilled Frank Knight on every aspect of his so-called investigation, his three-and-a-half years of surveillance, his biased interpretations of Palestinian culture, and his baseless conclusions about our activities.

It could have filled a book.

The essence was undeniable: Knight's testimony was riddled with contradictions. His observations were implausible, built on prejudice rather than evidence. His entire investigation had been shaped by ignorance, not truth.

Listening to him speak sent chills down my spine.

How could someone so uninformed, so detached from reality, hold the power to destroy lives?

How could a man with so little understanding of justice decide the fate of entire families?

It was terrifying.

And yet, the deeper realization was even more chilling: Frank Knight wasn't an exception.

Frank Knight Wasn't the Exception; He Was the Blueprint

Over the twenty years of the government's campaign to deport us, we met countless officials like him, agents, prosecutors, and bureaucrats who saw Arabs not as individuals but as permanent suspects.

Knight wasn't an anomaly. He was a reflection of a system designed to criminalize, surveil, and silence us.

But what Knight and his superiors never anticipated was our resilience.

They underestimated our unity, our defiance, and our determination to expose their lies.

They never expected that we would fight back, and that we would win.

The legal battle was intensifying. April 1987 became a defining month in our case.

The government began retreating from key charges, reshuffling strategies, and scrambling to contain the damage.

It was a month of legal chaos, but also a month of small, hard-earned victories.

Three weeks before our deportation hearing, the ACLU filed a lawsuit in the Federal District Court in Los Angeles challenging the constitutionality of the McCarran-Walter Act, the very law being used to prosecute us.

The case, ADC vs. Meese (later renamed as new Attorneys General took office), was backed by Arab American groups and civil rights organizations.

The lawsuit argued that our prosecution wasn't about security, it was about silencing free speech. It was selective prosecution, targeting us for our political beliefs rather than any actual wrongdoing.

ACLU attorney Hope Nakamura articulated the core legal principle: "There is a difference between advocacy of belief and advocacy of action."

Supreme Court rulings since the 1950s had reaffirmed this distinction, yet here we were, being prosecuted for our ideas.

Nakamura pointed out that the McCarran-Walter Act had rarely been used in decades, but in the midst of a "whipped-up frenzy against Arabs and Palestinians," the Reagan administration had found an opportunity to weaponize it.

National security paranoia had created the perfect storm for constitutional violations.

A Government in Retreat

Just one week before our deportation hearing, the government abruptly dropped the ideological charges against six of us: Ayman, Aiad, Naim, Julie, Bashar, and Amjad.

It was a stunning reversal. For years, they had branded us a national security threat, accused us of subversion, terrorism, and violence. But now, they were retreating.

The new charges? Mere technicalities. Visa overstays. Work authorization issues. Routine immigration matters that had nothing to do with terrorism.

This shift was a silent admission that we had never posed a threat.

Why did they drop the charges? Because they had failed.

After years of surveillance, infiltration, and propaganda, they had nothing to show. In open court, they couldn't prove their case. The ideological provisions of the McCarran-Walter Act simply wouldn't hold up under scrutiny.

But while six of us were spared, Khader and I remained under attack. As permanent residents, dropping our charges would have meant the government had no legal ground left to stand on. And they couldn't bear to admit total defeat.

So, they clung to the McCarran-Walter Act's ideological clauses, determined to pursue their original case, no matter how baseless it had become.

We were their "ringleaders." The organizers. The ones they wanted to make examples of.

Mark Rosenbaum of the ACLU summed it up perfectly:

"This is like the McCarthy prosecutions: they smear them, disrupt their lives, cry communism, and then don't let them respond to the charges."

The playbook was old, but the labels had changed. Yesterday's "communists" had become today's "terrorists."

The goal remained the same: destroy lives, silence dissent, maintain control.

A Turning Point in the Battle

ADC vs. Meese, our constitutional challenge, finally came before Judge Stephen V. Wilson in the Federal District Court of Los Angeles.

This wasn't just a legal fight; it was a battle for the soul of the First Amendment. A test of whether the U.S. government could criminalize belief instead of action.

At first, I was uneasy. Wilson was a Reagan appointee, known as a tough-minded conservative. I feared his political leanings would tilt the case against us.

But as the hearings unfolded, my respect for him grew. He wasn't swayed by political pressure. He wasn't playing along with the government's hysteria. He was interested in the facts.

On December 1988, the McCarran-Walter Act was declared unconstitutional. In a landmark decision, Judge Stephen V. Wilson struck down the very provisions of the Act that had been used against us.

He called it what it was: unconstitutional, a relic of McCarthyism, a tool of suppression masquerading as national security.

Civil rights attorney Steven Yagman put it best in the LA Times: "He [Judge Wilson] calls a spade a spade. He never makes a decision with fear or favor."

Wilson's down-to-earth nature set him apart from many judges. He refused to eat in the Federal Building's judges' dining room, preferring local fast-food joints instead. It was a small thing, but it reflected his humility and earned him quiet respect.

The government's efforts to prosecute us under the McCarran-Walter Act had failed, thanks to our legal team, the civil rights organizations that stood with us, and the resilience of our community. But the fight left scars.

Knight and others like him represented a system more invested in ideological conformity than justice. Their accusations were built on prejudice, not evidence. And though their case collapsed under scrutiny, the damage was done.

Our lives had been uprooted. Our families lived in fear. Our community was silenced by suspicion.

Just when we thought the government had exhausted its options, they made another move straight from their playbook of repression.

In a stunning twist during the hearing, they announced new charges against Khader and me. Gone were the accusations of subversion under the "communism" provision of the McCarran-Walter Act. In their place came a fresh set of allegations, crafted to fit the new political climate.

Now, under Section 241(a)(6)(D) of the same Act, we were accused of "advocating or teaching the unlawful damage, injury, or destruction of property."

Still, the McCarran-Walter Act. Still baseless. But now, reframed.

From Communism to Terrorism: A Convenient Swap

Instead of accusing us of being affiliated with an organization advocating world communism, they now accused us of belonging to one that "advocates or teaches violence."

The Cold War was ending. The "Red Scare" was fading. The new political bogeyman? Terrorism.

So, they swapped one buzzword for another, from "communists" to "terrorists," from "subversives" to "threats to national security." Same playbook, different enemy.

This last-minute charge swap proved what we had known all along: they weren't building a case on evidence, they were building it on political convenience.

They thought repackaging the accusations would make them easier to justify. They didn't care about the truth. They just wanted a conviction. But by shifting the charges so blatantly, they revealed their desperation.

In a rare moment of candor, Robert L. Bombaugh, director of the Justice Department's Civil Litigation Office, stood before the court and admitted the truth.

Judge Wilson was visibly displeased. He wasn't fooled by the Justice Department's maneuvering and wasn't afraid to say so. With controlled anger, he called them out in open court:

"I am frankly kind of piqued… that after hundreds of hours… you blithely tell us that you're not proceeding on the current charges."

Bombaugh conceded that the timing was "unfortunate." Among the reasons for the sudden shift, he cited "numerous press accounts" that had stirred nationwide outrage within the Arab-American community (Los Angeles Times, Ronald Soble, April 28, 1987).

It was a rare public acknowledgment that media pressure had rattled the administration.

Hundreds of hours of legal arguments. Years of government

surveillance. Millions of taxpayer dollars.

And now, at the eleventh hour, they casually discarded the charges, as if none of it had ever mattered. Even our attorney, Paul Hoffman, was blindsided, telling the court he had been informed of the new charges just "a few minutes ago."

For Wilson, a former federal prosecutor, the last-minute shift was unacceptable. Justice isn't supposed to be dictated by the media. Charges aren't supposed to change based on public relations strategy. His words cut through the facade:

"Changing signals at such a late date on the basis of the reporting of this incident by the media… seems not to be the format of the Justice Department I knew."

But Wilson didn't stop at condemning the government's tactics. He took aim at the law itself, calling the McCarran-Walter Act "over-broad" and "chilling."

He compared it to the McCarthy-era laws used to suppress dissent, and then posed a question that no American court had fully confronted before:

"The more important issue, which has never been settled by American courts, is whether or not resident aliens have the full panoply of constitutional rights, such as free speech, that U.S. citizens do."

For Wilson, this wasn't just another case; it was a defining moment. It was about the future of constitutional rights, about who America was and who it wanted to be.

He made it clear:

"I view this as the most important case that I've ever had."

Wilson's words reached far beyond our trial. He wasn't merely defending the Los Angeles Eight; he was defending the right to dissent itself. He understood what was at stake:

"We have people who were part of the community for a long time. They are participating in a dialogue, and that kind of dialogue is at the heart of our society. Nothing more important. And to take them and say, you're going to be deported because of a viewpoint, and that's all it is, a viewpoint, seems to be bordering on the outrageous."

Then came one last, powerful statement, one that has stayed with me ever since. Wilson invoked the Hyde Park soapbox tradition in London, where anyone, regardless of background, could speak freely without fear:

"On the Hyde Park soapbox… they should not have a sword of Damocles hanging over their legitimate political activity. We do have more and more resident aliens in this country, more and more people with different views, thank God."

Sitting there in that courtroom, I realized something profound: this fight was much bigger than us. We were at the center of a legal battle that could redefine constitutional rights for all non-citizens in America.

This was about more than deportation; it was about who gets to speak, who gets to belong, and who deserves protection under the law.

For the first time in this long ordeal, it felt like we had a judge who truly understood what was at stake.

Judge Wilson had called the government's actions for what they were: a sham, a disgrace, a violation of the very ideals they claimed to defend.

But the question lingered, would the system listen? Would justice prevail? Or would the government find yet another way to bend the law in its favor?

The fight wasn't over, but for the first time, the tide was turning.

On December 22, 1988, Judge Stephen V. Wilson delivered a historic ruling, one that would echo far beyond our case.

He struck down the provisions of the McCarran-Walter Act under which we had been charged, declaring them unconstitutional, a relic of McCarthyism that had no place in a democracy.

He affirmed a simple but powerful truth: free speech is a right for all, not just for citizens.

For the government, it was another humiliating defeat.

For us, for immigrants, for civil rights, for the principles of justice, it was a resounding victory.

The Los Angeles Times editorial on that very day praised Wilson's courage:

"Since it was passed over Harry S. Truman's veto in 1952, the McCarran-Walter Act has been a sore thumb of America's open hand to all people, creeds, and ideas. Finally, a courageous federal judge from Los Angeles has declared that crucial sections of this communist-scare legislation are inconsistent with the nation's constitutional principles of free speech."

This ruling wasn't just about us; it was about the country's identity.

Would America continue to suppress dissent in the name of security? Would the government keep punishing ideas instead of actions?

Or would the Constitution stand firm, even in the face of fear and political pressure?

The Selective Prosecution Case: A Victory for All

Our Selective Prosecution Case became more than just another legal battle; it became a defining moment in American civil liberties.

It reaffirmed that immigrants, like citizens, have constitutional rights. It underscored that the law must punish actions, not ideas.

It sent a clear message: the government cannot silence dissent by criminalizing viewpoints. This case wasn't just a victory for the L.A. 8; it was a victory for the entire country.

In a time of fear-mongering and political hysteria, Judge Wilson stood firm. He was fair, courageous, and true to the law, not to politics.

Although I never knew him personally, his decision left a lasting mark on my life and on the history of free speech in America.

"I will remember Judge Wilson's name as long as I live. He will always be a good part of my story."

Thanks to his ruling, our fight was no longer just ours; it became a fight for justice that would be remembered for generations.

At a press conference outside the courthouse, Khader Hamide spoke plainly and powerfully:

"They don't have a case. They are as confused as when they started, and they are trying to confuse the public as well."

His words cut through the government's shifting charges, last-minute maneuvering, and desperate attempts to brand us as threats. They had no evidence. No coherent argument. Only fear and propaganda.

We had denied all along that we were members of the Popular Front for the Liberation of Palestine (PFLP).

We supported their political agenda of liberating Palestine, their demand for refugees' right of return, and their advocacy for social justice, women's rights, and labor rights. We admired their principles compared to other Palestinian groups, but our activism had never been about violence.

Our attorneys proved in court that at least 95% of Palestinian organizations' activities within the PLO, including the PFLP, were political, social, and humanitarian. Military activities accounted for less than 5%.

Our work focused on political organizing, education, and cultural awareness, supporting Palestinian steadfastness in the face of Israeli occupation.

We organized lectures, theater performances, music events, photo exhibits, and film screenings. We used poetry and demonstrations to raise awareness.

We built alliances with Black, Latino, Asian, and Jewish Americans, churches, synagogues, and mosques alike.

We participated in Jesse Jackson's presidential campaign and supported the Rainbow Coalition. We believed in justice, not just for Palestinians, but for all oppressed people.

We were working to carve a space for Arab Americans within the American mosaic.

America, the Land of Immigrants.

Or was it?

CHAPTER FOURTEEN

THE MIRAGE OF INCLUSION
Arab Americans in the U.S.

We were here legally and peacefully, yet we were still seen as "other." Arab Americans remained excluded from the national narrative, unrecognized as part of the American fabric.

We were always viewed as foreign, suspect, outsiders, despite the fact that America was home to all of us.

After all, the U.S. has always been a land of immigrants, no matter who came first, except, of course, for the Native Indigenous peoples, to whom this land has always rightfully belonged.

Wasn't that the official American story? Or was it just a myth?

We never engaged in violence, never planned it, never advocated for it. Our activism was rooted in education, dialogue, and truth. Our tools were words, images, and community engagement. We were advocates, not terrorists. We believed in the power of discussion, not destruction.

When I immigrated to America, I was taught the ideals of democracy: a good citizen engages with national and global issues, participates in open debate, and contributes to the free marketplace of ideas. Democracy, I was told, depended on this. I believed it. I lived by it.

But when I practiced it, I was imprisoned. Labeled an "undesirable." Treated as a criminal, not as a good citizen.

What a letdown. America had preached democracy, but when

we actually participated in it, they tried to silence us. So, what was the truth?

Was America really the land of free speech, or was free speech only for those who didn't challenge the status quo? That was the question that haunted me. That was the question that defined my fight.

We, the Los Angeles Eight, embodied everything America claimed to value: civic engagement, democratic participation, and the exercise of free speech.

Yet instead of being celebrated, we were targeted, arrested, and silenced.

INS spokesperson Duke Austin went on record trying to justify the government's actions by stoking public fear:

"We don't have to wait until somebody blows up a bus or a plane before we deport them. We're not suggesting they be put in jail, we're suggesting they go home."

What a crock of nonsense. They had jailed us. They had tried to keep us in detention without bond. They had spent tens of millions of dollars trying to deport us.

"We're suggesting"? No. They were demanding. They were orchestrating a political purge, using deportation as a weapon against dissent.

After more than three years of surveillance, countless wiretaps, infiltrations, and secret reports, after deploying the full force of federal intelligence agencies, what did the government have to show for it?

We attended demonstrations. We carried anti-U.S. or anti-Israel placards. We planned fundraising events for humanitarian causes.

We distributed pro-Palestinian literature.

That was their case.

No violence. No conspiracy. No criminal activity. Just activism. Just free speech. Just the very things America claims to protect. And yet, they still tried to deport us.

They didn't fear us because we were criminals; they feared us because we spoke the truth. They didn't want to prosecute actions; they wanted to silence ideas.

They weren't targeting terrorists; they were targeting activists.

So, what did that say about the real nature of democracy in America?

The Deportation Hearing – April 28
By this stage, our case had split into two parallel legal battles: the government's deportation proceedings in immigration court, and our constitutional challenge in federal court alleging "selective prosecution."

Two sides of the same fight, each exposing the government's abuse of power.

From the moment I saw Judge Ingrid K. Hrycenko, I had a gut feeling, she leaned toward the government. She didn't seem neutral.

But even with a sympathetic judge, the government faced a glaring problem:

They had no case. No real evidence. No legitimate legal basis to deport us, at least, not until this hearing laid it all bare.

On April 28, the opening day of the deportation hearing, our attorney immediately raised the issue of due process.

We had been unfairly targeted. There was a blatant double standard. The law was being used selectively, weaponized against us, but ignored for others.

Leni Weinglass, one of our defense attorneys, presented a striking example of U.S. hypocrisy.

He introduced a declaration from a recent case involving Amy Carter, daughter of former President Jimmy Carter.

Amy had been arrested during a demonstration against CIA activities in Central America. In that case, Weinglass had called as a witness a man named Edgar Chamorro, a Nicaraguan national, Florida resident, and former leader of the Contras, the U.S.-backed paramilitary group waging war in Nicaragua.

Chamorro's testimony was explosive. He admitted that the Contras openly advocated violence and sabotage, and called for killing officials in Nicaragua.

And yet, not one Contra member in the U.S. faced deportation.

Standing before the court, Weinglass made it plain:

"If the government allows other aliens to commit sabotage in other countries, then it can't throw out these aliens for allegedly doing the same thing."

The U.S. was sheltering and funding foreign militants, while labeling us, Palestinians speaking out against Israeli occupation, as "terrorists."

The hypocrisy was undeniable. If you were pro-U.S. and engaged in real violence, you were protected. If you were pro-Palestinian and used only words, you were prosecuted.

The double standard stood exposed. The case against us had no basis in law, only in selective persecution.

Judge Hrycenko may have leaned toward the government, but even she couldn't ignore the contradictions. The truth was on our side.

Despite the government's objections, Judge Ingrid K. Hrycenko made a surprising ruling. She acknowledged the possibility that our due process rights had been violated but declared she lacked authority to rule on constitutional issues, shifting the burden to the federal courts.

Her words were direct:

"If any unconstitutional selective prosecution has occurred, it will not be in my courtroom."

Her decision astonished me. A former federal prosecutor who had seemed inclined to favor the government was now effectively washing her hands of the case.

It was clear she had taken note of Judge Stephen Wilson's stance in our federal court challenge and sensed the shifting legal landscape.

For us, this was a small but critical victory.

The deportation case was losing momentum. The constitutional case was gaining strength. The government's narrative was unraveling.

But one thing was certain, they wouldn't give up easily.

The Long War on "Evil Thinking"

Our case was not unique in history. The following are stark examples of repression by the U.S. government similar to ours.

Attorney General Edwin Meese III was not the first to target immigrants for their "dangerous" ideas, nor would he be the last.

Throughout American history, the government has used fear, nationalism, and "national security" rhetoric to silence dissenting voices, especially those of immigrants.

In 1920, Attorney General Mitchell Palmer launched a nationwide crackdown on suspected radicals. Using the Bureau of Investigation (precursor to the FBI) and Immigration Services, he orchestrated mass raids in 33 cities. Over 4,000 immigrants were arrested, many for nothing more than distributing "subversive" literature.

J. Edgar Hoover, then a 25-year-old special assistant, compiled a database of over 200,000 so-called "evil thinkers." Their crime? Challenging injustice. Criticizing government policies. Daring to think differently.

Another glaring example: Senator Joseph McCarthy's ruthless campaign against suspected communists. Lives destroyed, professions ruined, countless immigrants deported, not for crimes, but for beliefs. The government wielded ideological exclusion laws to purge dissenting voices in the name of "security."

Fast forward to 1987: The Los Angeles Eight Case, history repeating itself. Once again, the government sought to crush dissent. Once again, immigrants were targeted, this time, Palestinian activists. Once again, they accused us of "evil thinking," using the McCarran-Walter Act, a relic of the Red Scare.

My Journey of "Evil Thinking"

I immigrated to the United States in 1975, full of hope and ambition. Fresh out of high school, I came eager to pursue higher education.

I had spent my formative years under Israeli occupation, living in fear that expressing my thoughts could put my family in danger. America, with its Constitution and promise of liberty, seemed to offer the freedom I had always yearned for.

I fell in love with the ideals of free speech. I switched from engineering (my parents' choice) to journalism, I wanted to learn debate, critical thinking, and truth-seeking. I immersed myself in the First Amendment, embracing the "marketplace of ideas."

I pursued a master's degree in public administration, eager to contribute to my new home. I wanted to become part of the "American experiment."

Michel Shehadeh, 1975 – the year he immigrated to the United States

But when I practiced democracy, I became an "undesirable." The same government that taught me about free speech now sought to deport me for using it. The same country that encouraged civic engagement now punished me for participating in it.

I believed in America's promise, but America did not believe in me. When I embraced democracy, I wasn't celebrated; I was branded a threat. When I used my voice for justice, I was shackled, imprisoned, and targeted for deportation.

The real crime? Thinking freely. It wasn't about what I did; it was about what I believed. Because in America, free speech is only free if it doesn't challenge power, and I had dared to challenge it.

Most Americans believe in their right to free expression, enshrined in the Constitution. But in practice, that freedom exists within shifting boundaries. When the nation feels secure, voices for broader freedoms prevail. When fear takes hold, those freedoms contract.

Our case demonstrated how fragile liberty can be. As the saying goes, liberty is often the first casualty in war.

When a government wants to suppress speech, curb constitutional liberties, and justify repression, it needs public support. But how does it gain that support when its actions violate democratic values? It turns to fear.

During the Reagan era, when the Los Angeles Eight case began, America was experiencing a period of relative prosperity. Right-wing power was rising. Trickle-down economics fueled consumerism. The Soviet Union was collapsing, reinforcing the euphoria of Western dominance.

The United States stood as the unrivaled global superpower, presiding over a unipolar world order established after World War II.

But even at the height of its power, the U.S. needed a new enemy to replace the Soviet Union and communism. And it found one: terrorism.

All the government had to do was shout "Palestinian terrorists," and fear took over. They deliberately linked us to the "dangerous PFLP," knowing the groundwork for equating Palestinians with terrorism had long been laid.

For decades, the media and popular culture had saturated the American psyche with the image of the Palestinian as the ultimate villain.

No evidence was required. No coherent narrative was needed. Our guilt was assumed, not proven. And at first, the government's plan worked.

For the first two weeks after our arrest, the government's accusations dominated the headlines. The media parroted official statements, and anchors repeated "PLO terrorists," "PLO sleeping cell," and "terror suspects" without question.

The public absorbed the message. Fear took root. Support for repression grew.

But then something unexpected happened.

As the government failed to produce a shred of evidence, the narrative began to unravel. The same media that had once amplified the hysteria now began to ask questions.

Once the illusion of our guilt cracked, there was no putting it back together. The government had overplayed its hand; it had relied on fear, not facts. And when fear wasn't enough, the case began to fall apart.

The First Amendment is neither left-wing nor right-wing. It can be a tool for change or a shield for the status quo. It belongs equally to those who support Zionist Israel and those who advocate for Palestinian liberation.

For free speech to mean anything, it must protect everyone, without exception.

Our prosecution was about controlling the narrative, about deciding who gets to speak and who must remain silent. The government wanted to make an example of us, to ensure the Palestinian narrative stayed under Zionist control.

The case was meant to send a message: that advocacy for Palestinian rights was unwelcome, even dangerous. It was about creating a chilling effect, scaring immigrant communities into silence.

It was a zero-sum game, one that sought to render the very concept of free speech meaningless.

The First Amendment Was Meant to Protect Us, Not Silence Us.

The First Amendment was supposed to be a shield against government overreach, not a weapon for suppressing political dissent. It guarantees freedom of speech, religion, and the press; the right to assemble and petition the government, rights that belong to everyone on U.S. soil, citizen or not.

Yet, the government wanted to strip us of these rights, not just to silence us, but to intimidate entire communities. It was about shutting down any challenge to U.S. foreign policy, especially its unwavering support for Israel's military occupation of Palestine.

The Loss of Innocence

When I came to America, I believed in the promise of freedom. In college, I discovered the power of self-expression and learned that nothing is more dehumanizing than being denied your voice.

I began freeing my soul from the years of suppression I had endured under Israeli occupation. For the first time, I felt truly alive. I raised a family, worked hard, pursued higher education, and built a life here.

I thought my dreams were finally being realized in my adopted country.

But our arrest shattered that illusion. The feeling of innocence and belonging, the belief that I was part of this nation, was ripped away, never to return.

I believed being a good citizen meant staying informed, participating in democracy, and using my voice for justice.

I spoke out against U.S. involvement in Central America, apartheid in South Africa, inequality in education and healthcare, race relations, and LGBTQ rights.

But above all, I spoke out against the distorted portrayal of the Palestinian struggle for freedom and independence, an issue that wasn't just political, but deeply personal.

It was the defining reality of my childhood under Israeli occupation. It shaped my identity, followed me to the United States, and affected not just me, but my family, friends, and the broader Palestinian American community. For this, we were labeled dangerous.

The government arrested us, held us in maximum-security cells, and accused us of terrorism, not for any crime, but for our thoughts and ideas.

We were exemplary citizens, not even an unpaid parking ticket among us, yet we were treated like the worst of criminals.

The case was about power and the government's attempt to shift that power entirely in its favor by undermining the checks and balances of democracy.

The Bill of Rights exists to protect dissenters from government overreach. It was written not for the powerful, but for those who challenge authority, who refuse to remain silent in the face of injustice.

As John Locke, one of the great influences on the U.S. Constitution, said: "The end of law is not to abolish or restrain, but to preserve and enlarge freedom."

Our case was a stark reminder of how fragile freedom can be when fear is weaponized to erode it. Yet I still dream of a better day, not just for Palestinians, but for everyone.

My dream didn't die; it expanded. It became more inclusive, embracing all people struggling for justice.

The Shehadeh family, our Arab American branch, has taken root in the U.S., growing across generations. Today, I introduce myself this way:

"I come from Palestine, so I am 100% Palestinian. I live in America as a citizen, so I am 100% American. And my home is the Milky Way, so I am 100% a brother to everything."

Despite the immense toll the Los Angeles Eight case exacted, I like to think something good came of it. It taught me how to raise my sons with courage, how to stand firm in adversity, and how to walk the path of truth, even when it's the loneliest path.

Because when the rights of any group are threatened, the rights of everyone are at risk.

A Warning from History
Pastor Martin Niemoeller, reflecting on the rise of fascism in Nazi Germany, left a timeless warning:

"First they came for the Communists, and I didn't speak up because I wasn't a Communist. Then they came for the Jews, and I didn't speak up because I wasn't a Jew. Then they came for the trade unionists, and I didn't speak up because I wasn't a trade unionist. Then they came for the Catholics, and I didn't speak up because I was a Protestant. Then they came for me, and by that time, no one was left to speak up."

This is why we fight. Because silence is the enemy of justice. Freedom is not self-sustaining; it must be defended, protected, and fought for every day.

What happened to us can happen to anyone. The first victims of repression are always the most vulnerable, immigrants, prisoners, and the poor, but they are rarely the last.

When the government wields its power to silence dissent, it doesn't stop with one group. It sets a precedent. If no one speaks out, the circle of repression expands, ensnaring more voices, more communities, more lives.

Fortunately, in our case, the Los Angeles Eight, people did speak up.

Immigrant rights groups, civil rights organizations, churches, synagogues, mosques, politicians, and activists from across the political spectrum came together in solidarity.

On one side stood the government, bolstered by the Anti-Defamation League of B'nai B'rith (ADL).

On the other stood nearly everyone else, those who believed in justice, fairness, and the fundamental right to speak without fear.

It wasn't enough that the most powerful government in the world was targeting us for our political beliefs; it was joined by one of the most influential organizations in America: the ADL.

The ADL claims to be a civil rights organization, a defender of justice. But in our case, it revealed itself as something far different. Rather than opposing our persecution, the ADL worked hand in hand with the government to silence us.

Founded in 1913 to combat anti-Semitism and promote civil rights, the ADL once played a critical role in challenging McCarthyism and defending democratic values. But by the 1960s, something changed.

The ADL began aligning itself increasingly with Israeli foreign policy. The Six-Day War of 1967 marked a turning point. That year, it created a special "Middle East" department, not to defend civil rights, but to monitor, discredit, and undermine Arab American organizations and critics of Israel.

By the 1970s, it was labeling mainstream Arab American groups as part of an "anti-Israel lobby."

By the 1980s, it had become a central pillar of the pro-Israel lobbying machine, expanding its reach into intelligence-gathering operations against groups across the political spectrum, left, right, and center.

And along the way, it developed close ties with Mossad, Israel's intelligence agency.

CHAPTER FIFTEEN

THE WEAPONIZATION OF ANTI-SEMITISM

The ADL's greatest manipulation was its deliberate conflation of Israel with all Jewish people.

It pushed the narrative that any criticism of Israel was inherently anti-Semitic, that questioning Israel's actions made one an enemy of the Jewish people.

This false equivalence became a weapon used to silence critics, intimidate academics, and punish activists.

Arab American professors, doctors, journalists, and students found themselves under surveillance, blacklisted, and attacked simply for questioning U.S. support for Israel.

Our case was just one chapter in a long, calculated campaign to destroy dissent.

The ADL, which once stood against McCarthyism, had become McCarthyism, only now its targets were Arab Americans, Palestinians, and anyone who dared to speak for justice.

We were not the first to be targeted. And we would not be the last.

The Revelations of Spying

The ADL's direct involvement in our case was exposed in 1993, and the full extent of its surveillance was even more chilling than we had imagined.

That year, a criminal investigation into Tom Gerard, a former San Francisco police officer, unearthed a web of illegal information-sharing. Gerard had been selling confidential police files to a South African intelligence agent during apartheid.

In the process, authorities discovered that he had another major client, the ADL.

Searches of Gerard's property and ADL offices uncovered a trove of stolen police reports, fingerprints, driver's license photos, and dossiers, not just on suspected criminals, but on activists, civil rights leaders, and Arab Americans.

Among the files were documents on me, Khader Hamide, and others from the Los Angeles Eight.

The evidence confirmed what we had long suspected: the ADL had been running an extensive surveillance operation, infiltrating Arab American and pro-Palestinian organizations while working hand-in-hand with government agencies.

One of their key operatives, Roy Bullock, had spent over 32 years as an undercover agent for the ADL, posing as a pro-Palestinian activist, attending meetings, befriending organizers, and feeding intelligence to the ADL, which then passed it to Israeli intelligence and U.S. authorities.

For decades, the ADL had masqueraded as a civil rights organization while operating a private intelligence network that spied on critics of Israel and suppressed dissent in the U.S.

The revelations led to a historic 1993 lawsuit. Thirteen civil rights organizations and seven individuals, including myself and Khader, filed a federal suit against the ADL for violating our civil and privacy rights.

Albert Mokhiber, then president of the American-Arab Anti-Discrimination Committee (ADC), captured the irony:

"This is an unusual lawsuit. An organization that has done important civil rights work is being charged with violating civil rights."

The lawsuit stripped away the ADL's carefully crafted image and revealed the truth: it was not defending civil rights, it was weaponizing them to protect Israel's political interests and silence dissent.

Our victory against the government and the ADL was not just a triumph for the Los Angeles Eight; it was a victory for free speech, privacy, and justice.

It proved a powerful truth: when people unite, across political, religious, and cultural divides, they can challenge even the most powerful institutions.

The Los Angeles Eight case was a stark reminder that the rights of one are the rights of all. When we defend the freedoms of the most vulnerable, we safeguard democracy for everyone.

The lawsuit against the Anti-Defamation League (ADL) brought together an unprecedented coalition of organizations and individuals spanning racial, religious, and political lines.

These were not fringe groups or radicals; they were respected civil rights, legal, and social justice organizations with long histories of defending constitutional freedoms. Together, they stood against the ADL's covert campaign of surveillance, intimidation, and political repression.

This diverse alliance demonstrated a crucial truth: the fight against political repression wasn't just about Arab Americans. The ADL's spying operation threatened anyone who challenged U.S. foreign policy or stood in solidarity with oppressed communities.

Former U.S. Representative Mervyn Dymally, one of the plaintiffs, did not mince words about the ADL's tactics: "Whenever anyone utters any words deemed damaging to Israel or the Jewish community, the ADL is prolific in requesting an apology, which they are quick to equate with Nazism."

Former Los Angeles City Council Member Robert Farrell echoed the same: "It's obvious I was harassed for my support of Palestinian causes and the anti-apartheid movement."

At a press conference with Los Angeles City Hall member Robert Farrell, alongside Michel Shehadeh and attorney Brian Hudson

The ADL had transformed from an organization that once challenged McCarthyism into one that replicated McCarthyist tactics, targeting those who dared to criticize U.S. foreign policy or Israeli apartheid.

The roots of the ADL lawsuit trace back to a shocking discovery. In 1993, an investigation into former San Francisco police officer Tom Gerard revealed that he had been selling classified police files, not only to apartheid-era South African intelligence but also to the ADL.

When authorities raided the ADL's Bay Area and Los Angeles offices, they uncovered a vast spying operation targeting Arab Americans, Black activists, Indigenous rights groups, and anti-apartheid campaigners.

The seized files exposed the ADL's "fact-finding" program, an extensive, covert surveillance network designed not to combat discrimination, but to infiltrate, disrupt, and intimidate activists working for justice.

One name stood out: Roy Bullock, a longtime ADL operative who spent over three decades infiltrating organizations, collecting names, taking photographs, and handing over intelligence to both U.S. and Israeli agencies.

But his most disturbing deception was his infiltration of the American-Arab Anti-Discrimination Committee (ADC).

Infiltration of the ADC
Bullock did more than spy from the outside; he embedded himself within the ADC, posing as an ally.

He attended demonstrations, carried banners, and even pretended to be a friend to activists fighting for Palestinian human rights. Osama Domani, then the ADC's regional director, recalled the deep betrayal:

"He would come to my office, hug me in a comradely fashion, and volunteer for work. He wanted to be present whenever we had something important."

While Bullock embraced activists as a friend, he was secretly feeding their names, photographs, and meeting details to the ADL, which then passed them to the FBI and Mossad.

It was a direct violation of civil liberties, and something far more sinister: a calculated effort to undermine Arab American activism and suppress the Palestinian narrative in the U.S.

The ADL's invasive tactics went far beyond surveillance. Their operatives engaged in dumpster diving for documents, illegally obtaining police records, compiling blacklists of journalists and academics, and feeding intelligence to U.S. and Israeli agencies to stifle dissent.

The lawsuit against the ADL forced these operations into the light, revealing how an organization that claimed to fight discrimination had become an enforcer of political repression and U.S.-Israeli interests.

This wasn't just about us, the Los Angeles Eight, or about Arab Americans. This lawsuit set a precedent: if the ADL could spy on Arab Americans, Black activists, Indigenous rights groups, and anti-apartheid campaigners without consequences, then no movement for justice was safe.

It reaffirmed that political repression doesn't stop with one community; it spreads, threatening civil liberties for all Americans.

The fight against the ADL's spying operation was not just about holding one organization accountable. It was about defending the principles of free speech, privacy, and the right to dissent in a democracy.

And in that fight, we stood united, not just as Palestinians or Arab Americans, but as part of a global movement for justice.

Discovering that the ADL had spied on us, invaded our privacy, and even rummaged through our garbage was a violation unlike any other. It was an assault not just on our activism, but on our very sense of safety and dignity.

Yet beneath the anger, I felt something deeper, pride. Pride in standing alongside extraordinary activists and organizations, bound together by a common cause: justice for Palestine and beyond.

There was no mystery about why we were targeted. The connecting thread between every individual and organization spied on by the ADL was Palestine.

The Palestinian cause had united people fighting against injustice in South Africa, Central and Latin America, and across the United States. This was a universal struggle for human rights, and that was precisely why the ADL and its allies worked so hard to crush it.

We were not merely advocates for Palestine; we were part of a global movement for justice. The ADL and the pro-Israel lobby saw this growing solidarity as a threat. They sought to divide us, silence us, and punish us for our unity.

But they failed. Instead of breaking us, the government and the ADL awakened a giant. Civil rights groups, community organizations, and activists across the country recognized the danger of our persecution.

This wasn't just about Palestine anymore. If the government and the ADL succeeded in this case, it would mark a return to the darkest days of McCarthyism, when free thought was criminalized, and dissenters were blacklisted and silenced.

The fight had become bigger than us. It was now a battle to protect free speech, civil rights, and the very foundations of democracy. And that was a fight we refused to lose.

In 1996, after years of legal battles, the lawsuit against the ADL was settled out of court. As part of the agreement, the ADL was required to destroy the files it had gathered on individuals and organizations involved in the case.

It was forced to cease its illegal surveillance activities and fund a community relations program, a small but symbolic acknowledgment of its wrongdoing. The ADL also had to cover legal expenses, a further financial and moral defeat for an organization that claimed to stand for civil rights.

While we knew no settlement could erase the years of fear, harassment, and injustice, this was a clear victory. It sent a message: those who weaponize surveillance and fear to suppress justice will be held accountable.

The ADL lost that fight, but its agenda of silencing Palestinian voices in the U.S. continues to this day. The tactics may have evolved, but the goal remains the same, to suppress the truth about Palestine, delegitimize its supporters, and protect Israeli apartheid at all costs.

Yet with every attempt to silence us, the movement for justice grows stronger. The truth about Palestine can no longer be hidden. The voices of justice are rising, and no amount of spying, intimidation, or blacklisting will change the course of history.

CHAPTER SIXTEEN

THE JUDGE'S GAVEL AND THE CROWD'S ROAR
A Legal Turning Point

As we fought against deportation, a coalition of civil rights groups, legal organizations, and activists mobilized to challenge the McCarran-Walter Act, the McCarthy-era law under which we had been charged.

The American Civil Liberties Union (ACLU), the Center for Constitutional Rights (CCR), and the National Lawyers Guild joined forces in a federal lawsuit, ADC et al. v. Meese, filed on April 6, 1987, in the Los Angeles federal district court.

The case was more than a legal battle for our freedom; it was a fight for the soul of the First Amendment and the political rights of immigrants in the United States.

Presiding over the case, Federal Judge Stephen Wilson recognized its profound implications:

"…the court recognizes that this case has great importance not only to all aliens presently within the United States, but also to all citizens of the United States who desire to hear the views of these aliens…"

Judge Wilson's words cut to the core. This case wasn't just about us; it was about whether freedom of speech truly applied to all, or only to those whose views aligned with the government.

For the first time, a federal judge openly questioned whether immigrants had the same political rights as U.S. citizens. It was a moment of reckoning.

As legal and public pressure mounted, the government abruptly dropped the ideological charges against six of us on the eve of the ADC v. Meese hearing. But this wasn't mercy, it was strategy.

Rather than admitting defeat, the government pivoted. Instead of political accusations, they pursued minor visa infractions, working part-time while on a student visa, or overstaying a visitor's permit by a few days. It was clear they were grasping for justification.

For Khader Hamide and me, however, they clung to their explicitly political charges, shifting the language from "world communism" to allegations that we were affiliated with a group advocating property damage and destruction.

Despite years of surveillance, millions in taxpayer money, and the full force of federal intelligence agencies, the government had no evidence, none.

During our deportation hearing on May 8, 1987, our attorneys exposed the hypocrisy. We weren't criminals; we were being prosecuted for our beliefs.

To make their case, our attorneys called former Nicaraguan Contra leader Edgar Chamorro and Afghan resistance expert Professor Barnett Rubin. Their testimonies tore apart the government's double standard: Nicaraguan Contras openly recruited fighters and raised funds for war on U.S. soil. Afghan "jihadis" collected money for violent insurgencies. Yet none faced prosecution.

We, who had committed no crimes, were the ones facing deportation.

Despite overwhelming evidence of selective prosecution, the immigration judge refused to dismiss the case. The government was determined to prolong its persecution.

In response, our attorneys demanded to question Gilbert Reeves, the acting INS director in Los Angeles, who had signed our arrest orders in December.

We wanted to hear, under oath, the real reason we were targeted. Would he admit the political motivation behind our arrests? Would he acknowledge that this was about silencing Palestinian activism, not protecting national security?

The battle continued, but it was clear the government was running out of excuses. As the weekend stretched on, the weight of the coming hearing pressed heavily upon us.

This was no ordinary legal proceeding; it was a battle for truth, accountability, and the very principles the government claimed to uphold.

For days, we pored over documents, analyzed strategies, and prepared for every maneuver the government might use to obstruct justice. Our attorneys left no stone unturned, and our supporters doubled their efforts to raise awareness of what was at stake.

But beyond the courtroom, the strain was immense. For me, that weekend became a moment of personal reckoning. The endless uncertainty, the suffocating pressure of surveillance, and the toll of constant vigilance weighed heavily, especially on my marriage.

The burdens we carried, fear, exhaustion, and the unrelenting need to appear strong, were not just political; they reached into every part of our lives. For some of us, including me, they left lasting scars.

It was a weekend that tested our resilience, our patience, and our faith that justice could still prevail.

Even as we prepared, we knew the government would do everything possible to avoid placing Gilbert Reeves under oath. They had spent months dodging accountability, shifting charges, and manipulating legal loopholes to prolong the case.

Reeves' testimony was crucial because he had signed our arrest orders, a single act that could unravel the entire web of political persecution. If he admitted that our arrests were politically motivated, the government's case would collapse.

Judge Ingrid K. Hrycenko, to her credit, refused to play along. She wanted answers, and she wanted them on record.

The following exchange between Judge Hrycenko and Esmeralda Cabrera, associate general counsel for the INS, revealed how desperate the government was to avoid accountability:

Judge Hrycenko: "I have, since the issuance of the Order to Show Cause, tried to ascertain who signed the order. I have not been given an answer. I was told last week it is perhaps 99 percent, Gilbert Reeves. I am asking you, as an officer of the court and a representative of the government, to transmit my order that he appear in court on Monday, May 11, at 1:00. I don't want to take the chance if he decides not to. I'm not signing any subpoena. I want him in court, and I have stated the reasons for that. He should also bring with him the authority to sign the Orders to Show Cause."

Esmeralda Cabrera: "As I indicated to Your Honor yesterday, after discussing it with Mr. Reeves, who did indeed sign the Orders to Show Cause, he will be available on Monday. I cannot anticipate unforeseen circumstances."

Judge Hrycenko: "Today has been an unforeseen circumstance. On Thursday, I was told he was on leave, on vacation. I did not want to cancel his vacation. I was told he was available on Monday. Hopefully, there are no more unforeseen circumstances."

Cabrera: "Hopefully, yes."

This was more than legal maneuvering; it was evasion. The government knew that once Reeves took the stand, there would be no more hiding behind secrecy or shifting accusations. No more manufactured hysteria about "Palestinian terrorists."

It would come down to one man, under oath, forced to explain why we had been targeted.

When Monday arrived, the courtroom was packed. Supporters, journalists, and legal observers filled every seat, anticipating a moment that could change the course of our case.

Would Reeves appear as ordered? Would he tell the truth? Or would the government pull another last-minute trick?

We were about to find out. The hearing opened under an air of tense anticipation. Cameras clicked, journalists scribbled, and our supporters watched in silence as the stakes reached their peak.

Judge Ingrid Hrycenko, seated high on the bench, wasted no time. She turned to the government's attorney, Esmeralda Cabrera.

"Did you transmit my order, Miss Cabrera? Yes or no?"

Cabrera's voice was measured. "Yes, Your Honor. I did transmit the order."

"Thank you. Miss Cabrera, is Mr. Reeves in court?"

A pause.

"No, Your Honor," she admitted. For a brief moment, the room froze.

Judge Hrycenko's voice cut through the silence. "All right. I will terminate all proceedings for the defective issuance of the Order to Show Cause. No one has alleged or verified that Reeves signed the order or that he had the authority. All eight proceedings are closed."

The moment those words left her lips, "All eight proceedings are closed", the courtroom erupted. Cheers and applause filled the air. Supporters clapped, families embraced, tears streamed down faces. For the first time in weeks, the weight of fear lifted, if only for a moment.

Then, the government struck back.

Cabrera, defiant and cold, snapped, "Nothing changed. The cases are very much alive."

Alive? The judge had just dismissed them. It was a desperate denial of reality, an attempt to cling to control.

Before we could react, the courtroom clerk's voice cut sharply: "Everyone, be seated. The judge is returning to the bench."

Silence fell. What now? A moment ago, we had won. Hadn't we?

Judge Hrycenko reentered, her face composed but resolute. She turned to Cabrera, her tone calm but edged with finality.

"These cases are closed. That means terminated."

The air was electric, tension humming through every breath.

"Miss Cabrera," the judge continued, "before going on the record, I asked if Mr. Reeves was here. You stated, 'Yes, he's coming down.' He is not in court. The time is 1:22. I will no longer tolerate these tactics. Proceedings are terminated. Now, you may accept my decision or appeal. The choice is yours."

She turned to us. "Do the respondents accept my decision?"

Dan Stormer and Marc Van Der Hout answered without hesitation. "Yes… yes, Your Honor."

Hrycenko nodded, then faced Cabrera. "You have ten days in which to appeal. This hearing is closed. Again, for the record, all eight cases are terminated."

With that, she rose and left the courtroom. Just like that, it was over.

Or was it?

The government moved quickly, announcing they would refile the charges. Our victory evaporated into uncertainty.

As we stepped outside, a roar erupted from the crowd gathered beyond the courthouse doors. Supporters waved banners, chanted, and cheered. Cameras flashed as we raised our hands in victory, flashing the V-sign. Smiles turned into laughter, laughter into embraces.

For that moment, we let ourselves feel the joy. It was a victory, however temporary. But deep inside, we knew: the battle was far from over. The government would not stop. They would keep coming.

They would change the rules, move the goalposts, rewrite the charges, anything to win. But so would we.

After everything they had thrown at us, shackles, solitary cells, surveillance, secret evidence, deportation attempts, and endless prosecution, we were still standing. Still defiant. Still fighting. Still free.

Outside the courthouse, we stood together, a family forged in resistance. The weight of uncertainty lifted, replaced by a surge of relief, triumph, and defiance.

We had won, against all odds, against the full might of the U.S. government. The crowd roared, their cheers rising like a wave of solidarity.

Reporters pressed forward, cameras flashing, capturing what became one of the most iconic images of our journey, the eight of us standing together, hands raised in victory, living proof of resilience.

That photo became a symbol. Alongside Paul Conrad's haunting editorial cartoon, it formed a dual truth: one of triumph, the other of suffering.

The famous photo of the L.A. Eight standing with their spouses and friends after their first major court victory, captured in front of the immigration building, a moment of joy, relief, and collective triumph

The image before the federal building told the story of our unity and vindication, proof that we had withstood every assault and emerged unbroken.

Conrad's stark black-and-white drawing of shackled figures told the darker story, the injustice, the cruelty, the systemic repression we had endured.

Together, these images defined our struggle: one showing the chains they tried to bind us with, the other showing us breaking free.

Even now, when I look at that group photo, I feel its power. I see our younger selves, bold, unbowed, our hands raised in defiance. The laughter, the relief, the sheer euphoria of knowing we had won.

Yet that same photo is also a reminder of what we endured, the years of dehumanization, the government treating our lives like pawns in a political game.

But that day, before our families and supporters, we proved that truth is stronger than fear, and that no system, no matter how ruthless, can silence those who refuse to be silenced.

A Slick Move or a Sinister Ploy?

A government official later told the Los Angeles Times with smug satisfaction, "Was that a slick move or was that a slick move?"

The flippant remark revealed everything. Our lives, our freedom, and the very integrity of the justice system were treated as pieces on a chessboard.

It wasn't about justice; it was about winning, at any cost.

Our attorneys believed the government was maneuvering to replace Judge Ingrid K. Hrycenko with someone more compliant, someone who wouldn't question their authority.

Hrycenko had become a problem. She refused to be a passive participant, and her rulings infuriated the prosecution. A week earlier, she had overruled their objections and insisted on a due process hearing, something they claimed was beyond her jurisdiction.

Then, she questioned the authority of INS official Gilbert Reeves to sign the arrest orders, striking at the foundation of their case.

By daring to scrutinize their actions, she had violated an unspoken rule: judges were expected to defer to the government, not challenge it. For that, she had to go.

The full extent of their deceit became clear moments after Judge Hrycenko dismissed our case.

As our attorneys gathered their notes, still processing what had happened, ACLU attorney Mark Rosenbaum overheard a government lawyer gloating.

Turning to a colleague, Esmeralda Cabrera smirked and said, "She fell for it. This worked better than we thought."

It was a quiet confession, but a damning one. Her words revealed deliberate, premeditated deceit. The government had planned this outcome, predicting exactly how it would unfold.

They had deliberately withheld Gilbert Reeves, knowing it would force the judge's hand. They wanted her to dismiss the case so they could reinstate the charges and handpick a new judge, one more compliant with their agenda.

The Machiavellian Playbook

From the start, the government's tactics had followed a pattern: deceit, manipulation, and ruthless calculation.

They built their case on secret evidence they refused to disclose. They paraded us in shackles before the media, shaping public perception before we could even speak. They twisted laws, abandoning one set of charges for another whenever it suited them.

Their philosophy was simple: the end justifies the means.

Withholding Gilbert Reeves wasn't a procedural oversight; it was a calculated act, a betrayal of justice itself. They knew Hrycenko would have no choice but to dismiss the case, and they exploited that dismissal to engineer a fresh start with a new, more favorable judge.

Under growing scrutiny, government officials denied any manipulation. Yet, behind closed doors, a senior official told The Los Angeles Times a different story: "Judge Hrycenko was looking for a way to dismiss the case."

The audacity was staggering. Having orchestrated the setup, they now sought to rewrite history, blaming the very judge who had dared to question them.

Instead of admitting their deceit, they painted her as the one acting in bad faith, as though she had conspired to free us. It wasn't damage control, it was deflection, an attempt to preserve the illusion of fairness in a case that had been anything but fair.

Judge Hrycenko, dignified and composed, refused to respond publicly. She let the record speak for itself.

As we later learned, the government wasted no time regrouping.

CHAPTER SEVENTEEN

THE STUNNING CONFESSION

The very next day, the government issued a new arrest order, replacing Gilbert Reeves with Earnest Gustafson, the district director of the INS in Los Angeles. The move spoke volumes.

Reeves had been discarded. The government had lost confidence in him and brought in someone with more authority, someone whose title could lend credibility to an increasingly fragile case.

Gustafson was meant to restore legitimacy. Instead, he would become the man who unraveled their façade.

Years later, in February 1995, long after his retirement, Earnest Gustafson submitted a sworn declaration that shattered the government's narrative.

Under oath, he admitted the government had "singled out the L.A. 8 for deportation." With that single statement, the illusion of impartiality collapsed.

For years, we had said we were targeted not for crimes but for our beliefs. Now, a former INS district director confirmed it, under oath.

But Gustafson went even further. He revealed that he had signed our arrest orders under intense pressure from the FBI, an agency that had spent years investigating us, infiltrating meetings, monitoring our activities, and still found nothing criminal.

So, they turned to deportation instead, Plan B. When prosecution failed, they chose persecution.

Gustafson's testimony was devastating. He confirmed what we had always known: we were targeted not for what we did, but for what we believed.

"Had it not been for those affiliations, the INS and the FBI probably would not have sought to deport these individuals."

Those words, simple, direct, were a seismic admission. For years, the government had claimed this was about national security and immigration law. Gustafson exposed the truth: it was about silencing dissent.

He also acknowledged that cases like ours were almost never pursued by the Los Angeles INS office, one of the busiest in the country. Our case was an anomaly, an outlier, politically engineered from the start.

"There was no ground for their deportation other than their political affiliation and activities."

That single line captured the essence of our struggle. We weren't facing deportation because of paperwork or visas. We were being punished for our voices.

Gustafson's confession also exposed the power struggle inside the government. He described how, in September 1987, eight FBI agents stormed his office, demanding access to our case files, without warrants or authority. He refused, blocking their attempt to take over.

That confrontation revealed what we had long suspected: this was never an INS case. The FBI was pulling the strings.

Gustafson made it clear, this wasn't immigration enforcement. It was a political operation, directed from Washington, executed by the FBI, and rubber-stamped by the INS.

This was an intelligence operation, not a legal prosecution. In exposing the FBI's overreach, Gustafson revealed the deeper layers of the case.

The INS was merely a tool. The real architects were in the White House, the intelligence community, and the Justice Department.

For years, the FBI had surveilled us, infiltrated meetings, and tried to fabricate a criminal case. When that failed, they turned to immigration law as their fallback. When they couldn't convict, they sought to deport. It was politics masquerading as justice.

Yet, despite their vast resources, manufactured charges, and manipulation of the legal process, they still failed.

Gustafson's testimony revealed more than corruption in one case; it exposed a broader truth about the American justice system. His confession felt like something out of a familiar political playbook: former officials, once stripped of power, suddenly finding their conscience and revealing the truths they once buried.

It was a cycle we had seen before, bureaucrats seeking redemption, rewriting history, or cashing in with memoirs and interviews. Gustafson seemed to fall into the first category. Maybe age brought him clarity; maybe the weight of guilt had grown too heavy.

Whatever his reasons, his statement was invaluable. He had become our witness, an insider confirming everything we had claimed for years. His declaration was entered into the court record, finally giving our fight the proof it had always needed.

David Cole, our attorney from the Center for Constitutional Rights, understood its importance. "This evidence will ultimately be a linchpin in our claim for selective enforcement," he said.

This was more than a confession; it was irrefutable evidence that the U.S. government had weaponized immigration law to silence dissent.

But the government refused to admit defeat. When Judge Hrycenko dismissed our case on May 11, they immediately refiled new charges. Their tactic was clear, stall, delay, and wear us down.

This time, though, their strategy backfired. Frustrated by their conduct, Judge Hrycenko agreed to our attorneys' request for a hearing on whether the government had obstructed justice.

Her reasoning was simple: they had failed to produce Gilbert Reeves, the key witness she had ordered to testify, forcing her to dismiss the case. Now, by refiling the same charges, they were openly manipulating the system.

So, on July 23, 1987, the obstruction of justice hearing was set. The government's lawyers were livid.

Esmeralda Cabrera, the lead attorney, could barely hide her irritation. "Let's get on with these deportation proceedings," she snapped, dismissing the hearing as a waste of time. Then, turning to our lawyers, she sneered, "What are you scared of?"

It was a projection at its purest. We had nothing to hide. We were fighting for truth and due process. It was the government that had been caught obstructing justice, and now, they were cornered.

Then came a cynical aside from Bill Joyce, the INS deputy general counsel in Washington: "At this rate this thing is going, we'll get to the merits in 1989."

Even Joyce was frustrated with how long the case was dragging on. What none of us knew, not Joyce, not Cabrera, not even our own attorneys, was that this battle wouldn't end in 1989. It would stretch on for two decades.

At the time, we couldn't grasp the scale of what we were fighting. We were simply trying to survive, defending our rights, resisting injustice, and preventing our case from setting a dangerous precedent.

We didn't realize we were living a landmark civil rights struggle, one that would later be studied in law schools and remembered as a test of America's commitment to free speech and due process.

For now, all we knew was that quitting wasn't an option. And so, we fought on.

Leni Weinglass, our attorney, confronted the government's abuse head-on. His voice cut through the courtroom with precision and fury.

"The government is playing with my clients' lives," he declared. "That's why these proceedings have to stop now. It's making a farce out of a judicial proceeding."

His words carried the exhaustion of five brutal months, of endless hearings, shifting accusations, and a system designed to wear us down. But we would not bend.

Weinglass argued that restarting the hearings amounted to double jeopardy. Judge Hrycenko had already dismissed the case when the government refused to produce Gilbert Reeves, the key witness. Now, they were simply refiling the same charges, hoping for a more compliant judge.

It was a cynical abuse of power, a way to erase their own failure and start over, pretending the obstruction had never occurred.

"The government willfully wanted to terminate the proceedings that were going badly for them," Weinglass said. "And now they want to start again."

The courtroom fell silent. Every word landed like a blow.

Faced with the gravity of his argument, Judge Hrycenko took a bold step. She suspended the deportation proceedings, pending appeal to the Board of Immigration Appeals (BIA) in Washington, D.C.

It was a crucial victory. The government's misconduct was now part of the official record, and the case couldn't proceed until higher authorities weighed in.

Key questions loomed before the BIA:

Did the government intentionally withhold Gilbert Reeves to avoid exposing why we had been targeted?

Did they manipulate the judge into dismissing the case so they could refile it under someone more favorable?

And could we be forced to endure the same charges twice after they'd already been thrown out?

These weren't technicalities; they were questions that cut to the heart of justice itself.

Though Judge Hrycenko stopped short of dismissing the new charges, her decision made clear that something was deeply wrong with how the government had handled the case.

The battle was far from over, but for the first time, there was a glimmer of accountability, an acknowledgment that justice might yet prevail.

Now, the fight moved to Washington, D.C., where it would become a national test of civil rights, due process, and the government's power to silence dissent.

A Legal Odyssey

The deportation hearings were now in limbo as the case advanced to the Board of Immigration Appeals in Washington. From there, it could climb to federal courts in California, and, if necessary, all the way to the U.S. Supreme Court.

As the government reeled from its missteps, INS Acting Deputy Counsel Dick Joyce, in an unguarded moment, vented his frustration to reporters.

"Clearly, when we brought these charges against them, the L.A. 8, we didn't know we would have the Weinglasses of the world on the other side."

The bitterness in Dick Joyce's voice was unmistakable. He hadn't anticipated the strength of our defense, a formidable legal team led by Leonard Weinglass, one of the most respected civil rights attorneys of his time.

But what Joyce said next revealed the government's arrogance and desperation: "France got rid of 3,000 Palestinians, but we can't get rid of eight."

The comparison was chilling. To him, France's mass deportations were an example to emulate. We were not seen as individuals with families, histories, and rights, but as a problem to be eliminated.

And so, the ordeal dragged on, an unrelenting war of attrition meant to break us. The government knew it had no case, yet it persisted, wielding bureaucracy as a weapon to exhaust and silence us.

Every delay, every procedural trick, every refiling of charges was part of a calculated strategy to crush our resolve and send a warning to others who dared to speak out.

We had won another round, but victory never felt like triumph, only a fragile pause in an endless battle.

Still, we refused to surrender. We understood the cost of defiance, but the cost of silence would have been greater.

Because we knew one truth that carried us through every hearing, every cell, and every sleepless night: no government, no matter how powerful, has the right to silence those who refuse to bow.

CHAPTER EIGHTEEN

ANOTHER BATTLE GROUND
The Fight to Reclaim My Education

Continuing my education had always been at the forefront of my mind. It was, after all, the reason I had come to the United States. Despite the chaos surrounding me, I refused to abandon that dream.

In the fall of 1987, I re-enrolled at California State University, Long Beach (CSULB), determined to finish what I had started. But no matter where I went, the case followed like an unshakable shadow. I realized I would never again be just myself; I was now the Palestinian from the L.A. 8 case.

To some, I was a hero. To others, a threat. And to many, a pariah they preferred to avoid. My name had become a headline, my identity a controversy.

When I tried to register for classes, I was hit with a stunning revelation, the university couldn't find my file. No enrollment record. No grades. No evidence that I had ever been a student.

It felt like an erasure, as if an entire system had conspired to wipe me from existence. A place that should have been a sanctuary of learning had become complicit in my silencing.

This wasn't a clerical mistake; it was a symbolic exile. I had already been fighting the most powerful government in the world; now I had to fight for my right to exist as a student.

I refused to yield. I went from office to office, demanding answers. Each time, I was met with blank stares, evasions, and dead ends. It became clear that someone had deliberately erased me from the system.

With nowhere else to turn, I decided to confront the university head-on.

I walked straight into the office of University President Dr. Stephen Horn. The secretary looked up, startled.

"I don't have an appointment," I said firmly. "But I need to see Dr. Horn immediately about an urgent matter. Tell him that Michel Shehadeh, one of the CSULB students arrested by the government on charges of terrorism, is here to see him. Now."

Her eyes flickered with recognition. I had put everything on the table, daring them to deny me. If they wanted to erase me, they would have to do it to my face.

After a moment of hesitation, she said, "Be right back," and disappeared into his office. Two minutes later, she returned, her tone suddenly formal. "Dr. Horn will see you now."

I stepped inside to find a man in his mid-fifties, of medium height and build, dressed in a dark gray suit and red tie. His thinning hair was carefully parted and combed over, a small act of vanity against time.

He stood as I entered, extending his hand with a nervous smile. It caught me off guard; most administrators stayed seated behind their desks, radiating authority. But not this time.

"Mr. Shehadeh, how can I help you?" he asked. His voice was clear but carried a faint tremor, the sound of someone trying to project confidence while masking unease. He clearly recognized my name, though we had never met.

I shook his slightly unsteady hand and took the seat across from his desk. Every gesture of his, the polite smile, the measured tone, hinted at discomfort beneath a veneer of professionalism.

I thanked him for meeting me without an appointment. He waved it off with a courteous remark, perhaps to ease the tension, but I didn't intend to waste time on pleasantries.

"I'm unable to register for the fall semester," I said. "No one in the administration can locate my file. It's as if I never existed here."

He listened quietly, his posture stiffening as I spoke. I told him bluntly that I suspected more than a clerical error, that the university might have cooperated with the FBI's attempts to erase me.

"We are innocent until proven guilty," I reminded him, my tone steady but firm. He said nothing, but his face made it clear he understood exactly what I was implying.

Then I made my position unmistakable. "If this isn't resolved immediately, if I'm not allowed to register and my file isn't restored, I'll have no choice but to take legal action."

The room fell silent. He raised his hands in a placating gesture. "There's no need to escalate," he said, forcing a thin smile. Then, to my surprise, he stood and moved around his desk to sit across from me.

With no barrier between us, the atmosphere shifted. He seemed to want to appear conciliatory, perhaps even sympathetic, but I wasn't looking for sympathy. I wanted action, not words.

He admitted, almost reluctantly, that the FBI had accessed my records and that the university had complied because of a subpoena. His admission confirmed everything I'd suspected, yet I stayed focused.

Finally, he assured me I could register immediately. He would write and sign a note for the registration office and personally oversee the search for my missing file. That was all I needed.

I thanked him, stood, and made my way toward the door. He followed, maintaining polite formality. Outside, he instructed the secretary to prepare the authorization note.

As I waited, he offered a final handshake before retreating to his office, his expression unreadable. Whether he was relieved, resentful, or quietly sympathetic didn't matter. I had won, at least this battle.

The secretary, however, seemed less composed. Her face was tight, her demeanor uneasy, as though she disapproved of how the meeting had gone.

None of it mattered now. I had what I came for, the right to register, to reclaim my education, and to continue forward despite every attempt to erase me.

She avoided eye contact and said nothing. That didn't bother me. I wasn't there for her approval; I had achieved what I came for. Another small victory in a long, exhausting journey. For now, that was enough.

As I waited for the note, I couldn't help reflecting on Dr. Horn's nervousness during our meeting. I didn't understand it then, but later I learned he had political ambitions. It made sense; he likely wanted to distance himself from anything controversial, especially the L.A. 8 case, which had drawn national and international scrutiny.

Being seen as a government collaborator or complicit in false charges against his own students would have damaged his image. In academia, where freedom of expression is cherished and government overreach is often viewed warily, such a stain could be fatal to a political career.

Dr. Horn eventually left the university in February 1988 to

pursue politics. Five years later, he was elected as a Republican congressman for California's 38th District, serving five terms.

Once my registration was secured, I resumed my journalism studies, determined to reclaim some sense of normalcy amid the chaos. But life on campus was different now, charged, visible, and under a glaring spotlight.

Amjad, Ayman, and I had become reluctant campus celebrities. Our story followed us everywhere, whispered in classrooms, debated in hallways, and dissected in student papers.

The Uprising That Shook the World (Dec 8, 1987 – Sept 13, 1993)

Just as we were settling into the semester in late 1987, history shifted again. The First Palestinian Intifada erupted across the occupied territories, a raw, spontaneous uprising that shook the world.

It wasn't orchestrated by political elites but born from the collective anguish of a people suffocating under decades of military occupation and apartheid. The world called it the "Stone Intifada," a name drawn from its most iconic image, Palestinian youth facing tanks and rifles with nothing but stones in their hands.

Against helicopters and machine guns, they fought with courage, conviction, and sheer will. Their defiance electrified global consciousness. Those stones became symbols of resistance, of confronting an empire with nothing but faith and dignity.

The contrast was undeniable: occupier versus occupied, oppressor versus oppressed. The world could no longer ignore it.

But this was not the first uprising in Palestine's history, only the latest in a continuum of struggle. From the Great Revolt of 1936 against British colonial rule to the uprisings of 1947–48 against Zionist militias, every generation had risen against injustice.

The so-called "First Intifada" merely marked another chapter in an unbroken line of resistance, a movement passed down through generations, sustained by memory, endurance, and the unyielding desire for freedom.

What made the Intifada unique was its scale, endurance, and global resonance.

For six years, the uprising surged through Palestinian cities, villages, and refugee camps. It mobilized an entire generation and reshaped the course of Palestinian history, forcing the world to confront the reality of Israeli occupation in a way no peace summit or political resolution ever could.

The First Intifada was more than rebellion; it was reclamation. A people declaring, through their bodies and their lives, that they would no longer be invisible, that they would no longer mistake chains for peace. They would resist, no matter the cost.

It was a turning point for Palestine and the world alike.

Nearly a year had passed since our arrests, since the grueling deportation hearings began. The weight of it all was relentless, endless court sessions, strategy meetings with our attorneys, constant media requests, and speaking engagements across the country. Each day felt like walking a tightrope, balancing advocacy, exhaustion, and the need to keep hope alive.

Beyond the courtroom, life continued to demand everything from us. Our families needed our strength and reassurance. Our community, seeing us as symbols of both defiance and endurance, leaned on us for hope. And amid it all, there was school, the pursuit of a degree we refused to abandon.

For me, Ayman, and Amjad Obeid, continuing our studies was a quiet form of resistance, a refusal to let them strip away our normalcy or our future. Our plates were overflowing, but surrender was never an option.

A question lingered through it all: How would we continue our activism now?

We knew we would never stop; our ordeal had only strengthened our resolve. But the path forward was uncertain.

Then came the Intifada, a lightning bolt across the horizon. The defiance of our people, the courage of ordinary Palestinians standing unarmed against tanks and soldiers, reignited our purpose.

The uprising wasn't only resistance; it was revelation. It showed us that the struggle was larger than any courtroom, larger than borders. It was a declaration of life, of dignity, of a people refusing erasure.

It began in Jabaliya refugee camp in Gaza, after an Israeli military truck ran over and killed four Palestinians. That single act of brutality unleashed decades of pent-up rage. Within days, the rebellion spread across Gaza and the West Bank, cities, villages, universities, and refugee camps all rising together.

Palestinians faced tanks and bullets with only their bodies, voices, and stones, the simplest weapons of defiance. The world could no longer look away.

The roots of this eruption stretched back decades. In 1967, during the so-called Six-Day War, Israel's military captured the remaining Palestinian territories, the West Bank and Gaza Strip, bringing all of historic Palestine under its control. It didn't stop there, seizing the Syrian Golan Heights, Egypt's Sinai Peninsula, and parts of southern Lebanon.

Israel's dominance had been cemented, but so too had the suffering and unbroken resistance of the Palestinian people.

The occupation deepened. The settlements expanded. The repression intensified.

And then, in 1978, Egypt signed a "peace" agreement with "Israel", the Camp David Accords, and the Sinai Peninsula was returned.

But Palestine remained shackled, its people still fighting for the right to exist on their own land.

The Intifada was inevitable. It was the culmination of decades of pain, the natural response to a system that denied Palestinians their dignity, freedom, and future.

For us, watching from the other side of the world, it became the answer. The question was never whether we would continue our activism; the Intifada showed us how.

The Camp David Accords may have restored Egypt's sovereignty over Sinai, but they came at a devastating cost: Egypt was severed from the Arab resistance front, leaving Palestine increasingly isolated.

What had once been a united regional effort against Zionist expansionism fractured, with Israel's most powerful Arab neighbor removed from the battlefield.

Meanwhile, the Golan Heights remained under Israeli occupation, later annexed in brazen defiance of international law. In Lebanon, resistance forces continued to fight for their land.

In the West Bank, Israel's colonial settlements spread unchecked, tightening its grip while stripping Palestinians of any meaningful political agency.

For the Palestinian people, this was a bitter betrayal, but they saw through it.

They rose in revolt against the Zionist apartheid regime, rejecting its military repression and foreign domination.

Under occupation, there were no basic rights. No freedom of movement, checkpoints turned towns into open-air prisons. No freedom of speech; any expression of Palestinian identity was criminalized.

Palestinians lived under military law, while illegal settlers enjoyed full civilian rights. There were no civil, human, or economic freedoms, no rights at all.

This uprising was not just a reaction to decades of oppression; it was a demand for dignity, freedom, and the fundamental rights every human being deserves.

The Spontaneous Flame of Resistance
Without formal coordination, the uprising ignited across the land. Demonstrations erupted in cities, villages, and refugee camps.

Palestinians boycotted Israeli products and industries. Civil disobedience became daily resistance; workers walked away, shops closed, and students refused Israeli-controlled schools.

The people turned their very existence into defiance. And then there were the stones, stones against tanks, rifles, and a nuclear-armed colonial regime.

Day after day, Palestinian youth, some barely teenagers, faced heavily armed Israeli soldiers and settlers' militias. With nothing but stones and courage, they became the front line of the revolution.

These were not mere acts of survival; they were declarations of dignity.

Israel's response was immediate and brutal. The Zionist regime unleashed a campaign of collective punishment: curfews suffocated towns, mass arrests tore families apart, homes were demolished, and live ammunition targeted unarmed protesters.

Their goal was clear, to crush the uprising by any means necessary. But instead of breaking the Palestinian people, their brutality only strengthened the Intifada's resolve.

For the first time, the world could no longer ignore the reality of the occupation.

The myth of Israel as a democratic beacon shattered against images of soldiers gunning down teenagers armed only with their voices and their stones.

The moral bankruptcy of the occupation was exposed for all to see. After decades of being spoken for and silenced, Palestinians were finally speaking for themselves, and the world was forced to listen.

The First Intifada unfolded under Yitzhak Shamir, once branded a terrorist by the British in 1948 for his role in the Lehi (Stern Gang), a Zionist paramilitary group responsible for assassinations and bombings.

Now, as Israel's Prime Minister, he led a government determined to crush Palestinian resistance with the same ruthless tactics he had once used against the British.

At his side stood Yitzhak Rabin, the Defense Minister, architect of one of the uprising's most infamous policies: the "Broken Bones Policy."

Rabin ordered soldiers to systematically break the arms and legs of Palestinian protesters, often young men and boys, to terrorize the population into submission.

The policy led to horrifying scenes: children beaten in alleys, young men left with shattered limbs, entire communities traumatized by soldiers wielding their rifle butts like clubs.

B'Tselem, the Israeli Information Center for Human Rights in the Occupied Territories, later documented the staggering toll, over 1,000 Palestinians killed and more than 130,000 injured.

The violence revealed the extent to which Israel was willing to go to preserve its colonial grip on Palestine.

From across the ocean, we watched in horror as images of our brothers and sisters being beaten and shot filled our screens. The pain was visceral, the injustice unbearable. Yet even amid the brutality, we saw something extraordinary, a people who refused to kneel.

We saw children with slingshots facing tanks, women standing before armored jeeps without flinching. An entire nation rose in defiance against one of the world's most advanced militaries, armed only with courage, their bodies, and an unbreakable will.

Supporting the Intifada was no longer just an act of solidarity; it became the purpose of our activism.

The uprising ignited a fire within Palestinian and Arab American communities, sparking new waves of mobilization. Across the United States, Palestinians and their allies organized demonstrations, teach-ins, and awareness campaigns exposing the reality of the occupation.

But something deeper happened; the Intifada reached America's conscience. People who had never questioned U.S. support for Israel began to take notice.

Students, activists, and civil rights groups recognized the parallels between the Palestinian struggle and other liberation movements, from South Africa to the U.S. Civil Rights Movement.

The raw courage of Palestinian youth, confronting oppression with stones and steadfastness, cut through propaganda and silence.

For the first time, Palestinians were no longer just statistics or distant headlines; they were living symbols of resistance.

The Women of the Intifada: A Revolution Within a Revolution

Perhaps the most transformative aspect of the First Intifada was the central role of Palestinian women.

Long overlooked in mainstream narratives, they stood at the forefront, not only as participants but as leaders, organizers, and architects of resistance.

They didn't just protest; they built. Palestinian women led demonstrations, labor strikes, and boycotts of Israeli goods.

They established underground schools when classrooms were shut down, mobile health clinics to treat the wounded, and economic cooperatives to keep families alive amid economic strangulation.

Their leadership transformed the Intifada from a moment of defiance into a movement of social renewal, a revolution within a revolution.

They built parallel institutions that reduced dependence on the Israeli economy, creating foundations for self-reliance and long-term survival.

For them, the Intifada was not just a fight against occupation; it was a fight to redefine Palestinian society itself.

Liberation was not only about breaking the chains of occupation, but also about breaking internal barriers, claiming their rightful place as equals in the struggle and in the future of Palestine.

Despite the Intifada's complexity, Western media reduced it to decontextualized images: A masked Palestinian throwing a stone. An Israeli soldier towering over a child. Riots, burning tires, chaos.

The deeper meaning was erased. The media ignored that the Intifada was more than street clashes; it was a societal revolution.

It was the awakening of a people, the breaking of chains both external and internal, shaking off old paradigms and entrenched social orders.

That is what "Intifada" means in Arabic: to shake off. And Palestine had shaken the world.

The First Intifada was a cultural and social renaissance. It was when Palestinians, long oppressed and fragmented, reawakened their collective identity.

As the streets erupted with defiant chants, so too did Palestine's art, music, and literature. Theater troupes emerged, turning stories of occupation and resistance into powerful performances.

Muralists transformed blank walls into declarations of liberation. Poets gave new urgency to their words, their verses becoming anthems of defiance. Resistance became art, and art became resistance.

The uprising also fostered a return to self-reliance. Palestinians, subjected to economic strangulation by Israel, turned to the land for survival.

Victory gardens, defiant plots of cultivated land, sprouted in backyards, alleyways, and abandoned fields. Farmers reclaimed ancestral methods to produce their own food, resisting dependence on Israeli markets.

The act of planting seeds became an act of rebellion, a quiet yet powerful assertion that Palestinians would not be broken.

For us, the Los Angeles Eight, the Intifada illuminated our path forward. Amidst our own legal and political battle, designed to expel us from the U.S. and silence the Palestinian narrative, the spirit of the Intifada reached across continents and found us.

It reminded us that resistance isn't just surviving oppression; it's reclaiming agency, identity, and dignity.

Its resilience became our resilience. Its creativity became our creativity. Its unwavering determination became our unwavering determination. We didn't just support the Intifada, we saw ourselves as an extension of it.

Personally, the Intifada shifted my perspective on our fight in the U.S. I had always viewed the struggle against Israeli occupation in Palestine as separate from our legal battle here against U.S. government repression.

But now, I saw them as deeply interconnected, two fronts of the same war against colonialism, imperialism, and oppression.

The effort to erase, silence, and criminalize us in the U.S. wasn't just about deporting eight Palestinian activists; it was part of a broader campaign to eliminate Palestinian resistance worldwide.

It was all connected. The fight against occupation in Palestine. The fight against Zionist control of the narrative. The fight against the U.S. government's suppression of pro-Palestinian voices.

I realized then that Zionism was not just a Jewish colonial project; it was a Western one.

For years, I had focused on Theodor Herzl's modern Zionist movement, which began in Basel, Switzerland, in 1897. But now, I understood that Western Christian Zionism predated Jewish Zionism by centuries.

CHAPTER NINETEEN

STONES AND STATUTE
The Intifada's Echo in American Activism

The obsession with Palestine didn't begin in 1948 or 1897; it stretches back to the Crusades.

For centuries, Western empires sought control over the Holy Land, driven by religious zeal, colonial greed, and a belief in their divine right to rule its people. From the Crusaders to the British Mandate, to modern American imperialism, the desire to dominate Palestine has been unrelenting.

Zionism was merely the latest chapter in the West's long project of colonial conquest. Though the Jewish Zionist movement was the vehicle, the real power behind it was Western imperialism.

The British handed Palestine to the Zionists in 1917 through the Balfour Declaration, not out of concern for Jewish self-determination, but to secure Western control over the "Middle East."

The U.S. inherited this project after World War II, becoming the financial, military, and ideological backbone of Zionism.

The campaign to erase Palestinian history, criminalize resistance, and suppress pro-Palestinian activism in the U.S. was part of this system.

The First Intifada shattered the illusion that Palestine could ever be conquered. It proved that no amount of military power, political suppression, or historical erasure could extinguish Palestinian identity. As I watched the Intifada unfold, I knew:

Our struggle in the U.S. was just another battlefield in the fight for liberation.

The crusading spirit of the West never died; it evolved. Centuries ago, Christian Europe waged bloody campaigns under the banner of the Crusades, driven by zeal and a thirst for dominance over Palestine.

Palestine was never just a distant land; it was an obsession, a prize to be conquered, a foothold for Western ambitions in the Arab world.

Zionism was not an anomaly. It was the latest iteration of an ancient project, a colonial outpost in the heart of the Arab world, a Western garrison under a new name.

Zionism: A Western Creation

There have always been more non-Jewish Zionists than Jewish ones. Zionism wasn't a Jewish movement conceived in a vacuum; it was nurtured within the imperialist framework of Western colonialism.

It took shape within the same ideological landscape that birthed Nazism, fascism, and white supremacy, systems that sought to impose domination upon the world.

The Western powers who divided the "Middle East" after World War I also enabled Zionism's rise. They saw Zionism not just as a Jewish homeland but as a tool to entrench their control over the Arab world.

The Crusades used the Holy Land as a launching pad for European conquest. Israel serves the same function today, a military outpost, an armed extension of Western power, a settler colony designed to keep the Arab world fractured.

President Joe Biden's words expose Zionism's role in Western strategy: "You don't have to be a Jew to be a Zionist, and I am a Zionist."

"Were there not an Israel, the United States of America would have to invent an Israel to protect our interests in the region."

Israel is not just about Jews. It is an American project, a weaponized state built to uphold imperial dominance in the "Middle East."

Biden's words weren't an endorsement of Zionism as a Jewish movement. They acknowledged it as a geopolitical instrument, vital to U.S. global dominance, as crucial as military bases, oil pipelines, and puppet regimes.

The U.S. doesn't just support Israel, it uses it. As a proxy, a watchdog, and a justification for Western interference in Arab affairs. It keeps the region in controlled chaos, manufacturing consent for endless wars, arms sales, and military occupations.

For decades, the world was told that Israel was a safe haven for a persecuted people. But Biden's words exposed the lie. Israel was not a sanctuary; it was a fortress for Western imperialism.

It was never just about providing a homeland for displaced people. It was about securing Western control over a strategically critical region, ensuring no independent Arab force could challenge Western rule.

The very idea that the U.S. would have to "invent an Israel" reveals Zionism for what it truly is: A colonial outpost, a weaponized ideology designed to uphold Western dominance in the Arab world.

This is why Palestine remains at the center of global struggle. It's not just about one occupied land; it's about the entire colonial system seeking to control and exploit the Global South.

And that's why the fight for Palestine is, in truth, a fight for the freedom of all oppressed people, everywhere.

Biden's words strip away the illusions surrounding U.S. support for Israel. For decades, Americans were told the relationship was about defending democracy and Jewish security. But Biden's words expose a different reality: Israel is a geopolitical weapon, a military outpost serving U.S. imperial strategy.

This shifts the focus from refuge and democracy to the hard mechanics of power. Israel's purpose is not primarily to protect Jews, it's to safeguard U.S. hegemony in the Arab and Muslim world.

Behind the rhetoric, Israel serves as a military outpost, armed with U.S. weapons, crushing regional movements challenging Western control. It is a political enforcer, ensuring no Arab state dares to challenge U.S. interests.

Israel is a wedge, permanently destabilizing the region, preventing Arab unity. A laboratory testing new weapons and surveillance tactics on Palestinians before exporting them worldwide.

The U.S. doesn't just support Israel; it needs Israel. And that is the most damning truth.

The Intifada: A Shattering of Illusions

Living through the First Intifada, witnessing the will of Palestinian youth resisting one of the most brutal occupations, was transformative.

For me and many others, it was an awakening. We saw not just the courage of the Palestinians but the contradictions within America itself.

Support for Palestine grew on the streets, in student movements, and activist spaces. But in the halls of power? Unwavering support for Israel.

The U.S. government's response, more weapons for Israel, more cover, and more suppression of Palestinian voices, revealed the dual nature of American power.

On one side, grassroots resistance. On the other hand, the imperial machine. And between them, a widening gap that could no longer be ignored.

The Fight Against Zionism, At Home and Abroad

I realized that the battle we were fighting in the U.S., against censorship, surveillance, and repression, was not separate from the fight in Palestine.

They were two fronts of the same war. The same Zionist forces funding Israel's war machine were lobbying to silence Palestinian activists in the U.S.

The same power structures that enable Israeli apartheid were trying to deport us for speaking the truth.

The foreign policy of oppression and the domestic policy of suppression were not distinct; they were one and the same.

Our struggle in the U.S. wasn't just about defending ourselves; it was about exposing the machinery of oppression itself.

The Intifada and the LA8: A Struggle Without Borders

The Intifada was not confined to Gaza or the West Bank; it spread across every exile, refugee camp, and corner of the world where Palestinians had been scattered.

In the United States, it lived through the Palestinian American community, including the Los Angeles Eight. Our struggle in the U.S. became an extension of the Palestinian uprising against Zionist colonialism and for national liberation.

While Palestinians in Palestine confronted occupation soldiers with stones and unbreakable will, we faced a different but equally ruthless machine:

The courts that sought to erase us. The media that demonized us. The government that wanted to silence us. The Zionist lobby that worked tirelessly to exile us.

Every courtroom hearing, news interview, and protest we organized became another stone hurled at the forces trying to crush our voices. We fought the same war, just on a different battlefield.

The deeper we dug into our case, the clearer it became: Israel was not just another state; it was the West's colonial spearhead in the East.

It was not merely an ally of the U.S., it was an extension of American imperial power. It did not serve Jewish safety; it served Western strategic interests.

As President Biden bluntly admitted, "Were there not an Israel, the United States would have to go out and create one."

That sentence encapsulated what we had come to understand. The Palestinian struggle was not only against Israeli occupation, but it was against the imperialist systems that sustained it.

We knew that if we didn't tell our story, it would be distorted by Zionist propaganda, fearmongering Western governments, and mainstream media censorship.

So, we took control of our narrative. Despite the pressure of our legal battle, we fully immersed ourselves in the struggle to reclaim Palestine's truth.

We mobilized our communities like never before, challenging the Zionist grip on U.S. public discourse.

We exposed the brutal crimes of the occupation, not just through reports but through the raw, unfiltered stories of those living under it.

We disrupted the narrative that painted Israel as a democracy while it crushed Palestinians with its "Broken Bones Policy."

We forced the American public to see what was being done in their name, with their tax dollars, under their government's protection.

A Shift in Public Opinion

The images coming from Palestine were undeniable: Israeli soldiers breaking the arms of young Palestinians. Unarmed protesters shot in cold blood. Children beaten for defying their occupiers.

The cruelty was so blatant that even the American public, long indifferent to Palestine, could no longer look away.

Public sentiment began to shift. People began asking questions that Zionist organizations and the U.S. government had long feared:

Why is the U.S. sending billions to fund this brutality? How long will the world allow this to continue? The shield of unquestioning support for Israel began to crack.

We rode this wave and helped lead it. In Southern California, across the U.S., and even on the national stage, we stood at the forefront of a growing movement for Palestine.

We were no longer just defending ourselves from deportation. We were carrying forward the voices of the oppressed, the voices of the Intifada, the voices of an occupied people demanding their freedom.

This was a battle not just for justice in the courts, but for justice in the hearts and minds of the people. We seized the moment.

As part of the Committee for a Democratic Palestine (CDP), the progressive student wing of the General Union of Palestine Students (GUPS), we organized protests, seminars, film series, and theater performances that brought the Palestinian story to life.

We flew in Palestinian musicians and artists, their melodies weaving the heartbeat of a people refusing to be silenced.

The response was beyond our imagination. Crowds swelled. Engagement deepened. People were listening. The walls of indifference and fear began to crumble.

For the first time, the Palestinian cause, long distorted or ignored, was truly heard in spaces we'd never reached.

The FBI lurked at our events, but instead of fear, we welcomed their presence. We wanted them to see our unbreakable spirit, our defiance, and our growing movement. We were here, and we were not afraid.

Everything we did was legal, protected by the Constitution. As momentum built, the fear that had gripped our community dissolved.

The hesitation, the reluctance, the anxiety, melted away. People no longer feared standing with us or raising their voices for Palestine.

Then came December 1987, the Palestine Day Festival in Los Angeles. Over a thousand Palestinians gathered, the largest event of its kind. And something unforgettable happened.

We, the Los Angeles Eight, were called to the stage. As we stepped forward, the room erupted. A standing ovation, loud and overwhelming.

It was more than applause; it was a declaration that we were no longer outcasts, no longer whispered about. We were embraced as heroes of the cause.

I still have a picture from that night. The eight of us, standing together, victorious, not because the legal battle was over, but because we had refused to break.

The L.A. Eight standing together on stage, welcomed by the community at a public event

That photograph is a testament to the fight, the journey, and the bond between our people and us.

For the first time in decades, the Palestinian people, wherever they were in the world, felt unified.

From refugee camps to Gaza and the West Bank, to exiled communities worldwide, we were one.

The slogan "No voice is louder than the voice of the Intifada" wasn't just a chant; it was the truth. No faction, no ideology, no division, just one people, rising together, believing liberation was within reach.

The Dream of a Free Palestine

For the first time, we truly believed that the tide was turning. The dream of an independent Palestinian state, of self-determination, of justice, was no longer distant; it was imminent. Hope surged like never before.

It pulsed through the streets of Palestine and echoed in the voices of exiles worldwide. We were no longer just surviving; we were on the brink of winning.

Palestinian students stood at the heart of the Intifada, not just as demonstrators but as architects of the movement. They carried its energy and defiance into classrooms, until those classrooms were taken from them.

Recognizing the power of an educated, politically conscious generation, Israel turned its military aggression toward Palestinian academic institutions.

Universities and schools became battlegrounds, targeted with closures, raids, and systemic repression. Soldiers stormed lecture halls, arrested professors, and fired tear gas into student-filled courtyards. Education, the very act of learning, became a crime.

Yet, the Palestinian people met this assault not with surrender but with innovation, creativity, and resistance.

When Israeli forces shut down Palestinian universities, students and educators refused to be silenced.

They created underground schools, holding lectures in private homes, mosques, and community centers. Informal education networks emerged, ensuring that knowledge continued despite the occupation's efforts to suppress it.

This was no longer just education. Every hidden classroom, every whispered lecture, every smuggled textbook became an act of defiance.

By persisting in their pursuit of knowledge, Palestinians sent a message louder than any street protest: you can close our universities, but you will never erase our minds.

Bringing the Struggle to U.S. Campuses

In the U.S., as part of the Committee for Democratic Palestine (CDP), we knew that the fight for Palestinian academic freedom could expose the suffering under Israeli occupation.

We believed that bringing this struggle to American campuses would awaken new audiences to the reality of life under occupation.

Thus, the Palestinian Academic Freedom Campaign was born. Its goals were urgent:

- Reopen Palestinian Universities: Pressure Israel to lift closures and allow Palestinian institutions to function freely.
- Sister University Relationships: Establish partnerships between U.S. and Palestinian universities, fostering solidarity and exchange.

Mazen Jirbawi, Michel Shehadeh, and Omar Barghouti leading the opening session at the "Re-Open Palestinian Universities" Conference in Washington, D.C., in the late 1980s

I poured my energy into these efforts, taking leadership roles locally and nationally. To strengthen the movement, I developed a campus organizing manual, a blueprint for pro-Palestinian activism.

This manual was adopted by CDP and GUPS chapters across the country, guiding students to mobilize support, organize actions, and advocate for Palestinian rights.

A major victory came in 1991 when California State University, Long Beach (CSULB), my university, became the first American school to establish a sister university relationship with Birzeit University in the West Bank. This was a groundbreaking achievement, marking formal recognition of the academic repression in Palestine.

The Palestinian Academic Freedom Campaign, launched in Fall 1988, ignited activity across U.S. campuses. At CSULB, we founded Students and Faculty to Reopen Palestinian Universities, uniting students and professors in the fight for Palestinian academic freedom.

Michel Shehadeh and Professor Sherna Gluck, with members of Students and Faculty to Reopen Palestinian Universities, are campaigning and demonstrating for Palestinian academic freedom

My co-founder, Professor Sherna Gluck, a Jewish professor and lifelong champion for Palestinian liberation, became the group's faculty advisor. Her solidarity and support were unwavering.

Together, we bridged the gap between academia and activism, showing that the fight for Palestinian freedom was a moral imperative, transcending race, religion, and background.

This collaboration, Palestinian and non-Palestinian, Arab and Jewish, activist and scholar, became a model for campuses nationwide.

As the campaign spread, it amplified the Palestinian struggle through education and intellectual freedom, cutting through propaganda and speaking to the core values of universities: the right to think, question, and learn.

Some fight with stones. Some fight with words. Some fight with ideas. We fought on all fronts.

In this fight, we found a new battlefield, one where the weapons were knowledge, solidarity, and an unrelenting demand for justice. And we were winning.

Bridging Two Worlds: Birzeit and CSULB

From the start, we knew direct engagement with Birzeit University's students and faculty was essential.

This wasn't just advocacy; it was about building bridges, forging connections, and amplifying the voices of those living under occupation.

One of the most powerful aspects of our campaign was organizing visits from Birzeit faculty and students to CSULB.

They came as living testaments to the resilience of Palestinian academia, not distant figures in an abstract struggle. Their lectures, discussions, and firsthand testimonies cut through propaganda, offering an unfiltered truth about life under Israeli occupation.

Every story shared, every classroom discussion held, shattered misconceptions and deepened understanding, not just among students, but faculty, administrators, and even the skeptical or indifferent.

We also curated an influential speaker series, bringing respected voices in the Palestinian and pro-Palestinian movements to CSULB.

Among them was Dr. Naseer Aruri, a towering intellectual and Professor dedicated to Palestinian liberation, and Dr. Elaine Hagopian, a distinguished Syrian American professor who shared insights on Palestinian oppression.

We invited Hilton Obenzinger, an anti-Zionist Jewish professor, whose presence reminded us that Zionism is not synonymous with Judaism and that many courageous Jewish voices stand against Israeli apartheid, Zionism, and for Palestinian liberation.

These events were more than lectures; they were transformative moments that shifted perspectives and deepened commitment.

Each seminar and discussion chipped away at the distorted narrative that had long defined public discourse on Palestine.

To expand our reach, we worked closely with political science professors to present directly to their students. Sometimes addressing a single class, other times filling large lecture halls, these became vibrant spaces for seminars, film screenings, and panel discussions.

The impact was immeasurable. Students who had never critically examined Palestine found themselves confronted with history and perspectives they had never encountered.

Of course, Zionist students challenged us aggressively, but we welcomed their presence. Their opposition only fueled the conversation, drawing in more students eager to hear both sides.

In every debate, we stood firm, not because we were more eloquent, but because history, logic, and the undeniable truth of our cause were on our side.

With each argument dismantled, we saw more students begin to question the pro-Israel narrative they had been fed for years.

We weren't just winning arguments; we were winning minds. To amplify our message, we brought in prominent Arab American figures, including Casey Kasem.

Casey was a cultural bridge, able to speak to mainstream American audiences while championing Palestinian justice. His participation drew significant media attention, expanding our reach beyond activist circles.

With each event and debate, we reclaimed the Palestinian narrative from Zionist distortion. Palestine was no longer a footnote in someone else's story; it would be told on our terms, by our voices, through our lived experiences.

We weren't just educating, we were awakening. We weren't just fighting for Palestine, we were reshaping the way Palestine was understood in America.

And there was no turning back. Our cultural events on campus were electric, inclusive, and unforgettable, each one a bridge between Palestinian heritage and other communities.

One of my favorites was "Salsa for Palestine", a fusion of Mexican and Palestinian culture embodying solidarity, resilience, and shared struggle.

The event was a sensory feast, spiced falafel and sizzling tacos, knafeh and Tres leches cake, olive oil and salsa verde. Salsa rhythms intertwined with Palestinian beats, creating an infectious energy that kept everyone on their feet.

Salsa for Palestine Event Flyer at CSULB

The flyer remains a cherished keepsake, depicting a humanized jalapeño with a Palestinian kuffiya, shaking maracas and beating a tumba drum, dancing to the rhythm of revolution.

That night, barriers dissolved. The shared struggles of Palestinians and Latin Americans, against colonialism, oppression, and displacement, were vividly clear.

The event was a collective effort, supported by student organizations that saw their struggles reflected in ours.

La Raza Student Association, International Student Association, Folkorista Del Pueblo, Iranian Student Union, General Union of Palestine Students, Students for Peace & Justice, and the Palestine Solidarity Committee all proudly joined forces with us. Even Associated Students (AS), our student government, endorsed it.

Then, a moment of pure magic: I took the stage and wrapped my kuffiya around Zachary Williams, the Black president of Associated Students (AS). He wore it with pride, understanding its meaning, and spoke words filled with conviction and truth.

He linked the Palestinian struggle to Black liberation, anti-apartheid resistance, and every fight for justice worldwide. The crowd roared, the energy surged, and for a moment, we weren't just students, we were a movement.

Then, the music took over. King King Allstars, a powerhouse Latin band, kept the energy soaring. Students ate, danced, and celebrated, their joy echoing through the space.

That night wasn't just entertainment; it was a political statement. We had made Palestine impossible to ignore.

FROM CSULB TO COLUMBIA
A Legacy of Resistance

With momentum behind us and the campus community energized, we knew it was time to take our cause to the highest governing body on campus: the CSULB Academic Senate. This wasn't just symbolic; it was a demand for institutional action.

We wanted CSULB to officially adopt a sister university relationship with Birzeit University, solidifying our commitment to Palestinian education. It was the culmination of years of organizing, educating, and breaking down walls.

On December 7, 1989, we stood before the CSULB Academic Senate for a formal debate and vote on two resolutions:

- A resolution in support of Palestinian academic freedom.
- A motion to establish a sister university relationship between CSULB and Birzeit University.

This was the moment where our struggle, resilience, and refusal to be silenced would either be recognized or denied. We weren't just speaking for ourselves; we were speaking for every Palestinian student, teacher, and professor silenced, displaced, or oppressed under occupation.

This achievement wasn't the work of a few; it was the triumph of a collective force: faculty, students, and community allies who refused to be silenced.

At the heart of our movement was Professor Sherna Gluck, our advisor and a fearless advocate for justice. Alongside her were faculty allies like Professor Alan Lowenthal, who helped us navigate institutional channels with wisdom and conviction.

Student leaders like Zach Williams, President of Associated Students (AS), and Christina Speakers, the AS Vice President, stood unwaveringly by our side. Their leadership helped transform a grassroots movement into a campus-wide force for change.

In the spring, the CSULB Associated Students Senate had already passed a resolution supporting the sister university relationship with Birzeit University. The foundation was laid. The students were with us. Now, it was time to take the fight to the CSULB Academic Senate.

A Nationwide Struggle for Palestine

Meanwhile, across the country at the University of Wisconsin, Madison, another battle unfolded. Students had advocated for a sister university relationship with An-Najah University in Nablus, Palestine.

But under immense pressure from the Zionist lobby, the Wisconsin Student Senate was forced to rescind the resolution, dealing a blow to their campaign. This was a stark reminder of the power of pro-Israel pressure groups and the lengths they would go to silence Palestinian advocacy.

We knew this fight wasn't just ours; it was part of a global struggle. So, we reached out to Zach Williams and urged him to write a letter of solidarity to the University of Wisconsin Student Senate. Without hesitation, he agreed. His letter reminded them that resistance continues, even in the face of intimidation, and that they weren't alone.

We had spent weeks organizing and rallying support, knowing this wasn't just another meeting; it was a moment in history.

Before the Academic Senate convened, we held a vigil in front of the University Bookstore. Students, faculty, and supporters gathered in solemn unity, sending a message of defiance. The timing was perfect.

That morning, the Daily Forty-Niner, CSULB's student newspaper, published an article about our campaign, ensuring that every senator in the room knew what was at stake before casting their vote.

As we walked toward the meeting hall, we felt the weight of the moment pressing upon us. This was it.

Everything we had fought for, all the work and sacrifices, had led to this night.

Would CSULB stand on the right side of history? Would we finally achieve the institutional recognition Palestine deserved? The room was packed, and the tension was thick. The debate began.

Professor Alan Lowenthal introduced the resolution, stating to the Daily Forty-Niner, "We see it as a straightforward question of academic freedom." His words cut through the noise. This wasn't about politics or ideology; it was about the fundamental right to education, the right of Birzeit University's students and faculty to pursue knowledge, free from military closures and repression.

The Debate: A Night to Remember

What followed was an extraordinary debate. Every time I reflect on it, I feel the same surge of pride. It was one of those rare moments where everything aligned, the energy, conviction, and unstoppable momentum of justice in action.

The discussion centered on whether the resolution was political advocacy or a stand for academic freedom. The arguments were fierce, but the truth was on our side. As the deliberations stretched on, the tide was clear, we were winning.

Then came the final vote: a landslide victory. Fifty in favor, one against.

The lone dissenting senator offered a weak objection, wanting "a record of opposition." It was meaningless, a symbolic gesture in a historic moment.

Shortly after, the agreement was signed, formalizing the sister university relationship between CSULB and Birzeit University.

A Historic Signing, A Historic Victory

The agreement was signed by: Dr. Robert Maxon, CSULB President; Dr. Karl Anatol, Provost; Dr. Paul Lewis, Director of the Center for International Education; and on behalf of Birzeit University, Dr. Hanna Nasir, President, and Dr. Ibrahim Abu-Lughod, Vice President.

With one stroke of a pen, our struggle became a groundbreaking achievement. This wasn't just an institutional agreement; it was an act of solidarity.

It sent a message to the world that Palestinian academic institutions mattered, that their closure under occupation was an outrage that could not be ignored.

CSULB became the only American university to establish a sister relationship with a Palestinian institution. It was a small but meaningful contribution to the Intifada, a way to say, "You are not alone."

It was a victory for academic freedom, solidarity, and justice.

UNLV, 1989, Breaking the Silence

In 1989, as a journalism student at Cal State Long Beach, I traveled to the University of Nevada, Las Vegas, to attend a national student leadership conference. I arrived with questions and conviction, eager to connect, to learn, and to contribute. It was arranged that I would meet another Palestinian student activist, Hatem Bazian, who had come from the Bay Area. That weekend not only marked the beginning of a lifelong friendship with the now Professor Bazian of UC Berkeley, but also witnessed a historic milestone in the American student movement for Palestine.

The conference convened student government leaders from across the country. For the first time, a resolution supporting Palestinian rights was introduced at the United States Student Association (USSA). The proposal was straightforward, principled, and immediately contested. What had long been excluded from the conversation was now being brought to the floor.

The backlash was swift and coordinated. Delegates aligned with pro-Israel interests used every tactic at their disposal to block the vote: procedural filibusters, pulled fire alarms, and even attempts to shut down the building under a pretext. But this time, the momentum was with us. A strong delegation from the East Coast, particularly from CUNY, stood their ground. Many were students of color, determined to challenge a status quo that had long erased their narratives and silenced solidarity.

Hatem's mastery of parliamentary procedure became our greatest defense. With sharp focus and calm precision, he deflected each obstruction, opening space for honest debate and principled resolution. I worked alongside him and others to build coalitions, keep morale strong, and ensure we reached the vote.

When the vote finally came, the result was overwhelming: the resolution passed with broad support. Fewer than twenty delegates stood in opposition. It was more than a procedural win; it was a crack in the silence. For the first time, Palestine had entered the official discourse of a major U.S. student body. We weren't just advocating policy, we were making space for a people, a history, and a truth too long ignored.

That moment in Las Vegas became an anchor in my memory. It taught me that resistance doesn't always come in sweeping gestures; it can rise from careful preparation, shared purpose, and an unshakable belief in justice. The bond formed with Hatem that weekend became a constant thread throughout the years that followed. And the lesson learned, that when rooted in truth and solidarity, even the most hostile spaces can be bent toward justice, has stayed with me ever since.

Today, in 2025, the energy on U.S. campuses, students standing in solidarity with Palestine, fearless voices rising against injustice, feels like history repeating itself.

The echoes of 1988 at CSULB and the 1989 UNLV Student Conference are unmistakable. Then, as now, the government and Zionist forces sought to silence us through arrests, deportation threats, and efforts to block Palestinian voices from reaching American ears. Today, they repeat the same playbook: government crackdowns, surveillance, and coordinated attempts to suppress pro-Palestinian voices across the country.

The recent arrest of Columbia University student Mahmoud Khalil and the attempt to deport him for pro-Palestinian advocacy is the latest effort to criminalize dissent.

Just as they tried to erase us, they are now trying to erase this new generation of activists, intimidating them into silence, making them believe speaking out comes at too great a cost.

But something is different this time. The seeds we planted in the 1980s and 1990s have grown into an unshakable force.

The resistance on campuses is no longer a whisper; it is a roar. Despite arrests, crackdowns, and deportations, young people refuse to be silenced. They see through the propaganda and stand firm in the face of intimidation.

And that is the greatest victory. The struggle for Palestine is no longer just a movement for a few activists; it spans generations, woven into global solidarity. The resilience and passion of today's students prove that the fight for justice never fades; it only grows stronger.

In June 1990, I stood among my fellow graduates at California State University, Long Beach. This moment should have been a triumphant conclusion, but for me, it was more than academia; it was a defiant victory over obstacles and injustice.

As I stepped forward to receive my bachelor's degree in Magazine Journalism, I wasn't just completing my studies. I was a Palestinian fighter in the battle for existence, a father striving for a future, a man refusing to be broken.

A Kufiyah and a Diploma: Symbols of Two Struggles

Draped over my gown was a black-and-white Kufiyah, woven with history, struggle, and resilience. It wasn't just an accessory; it was a declaration. Even in the face of oppression and attempts to erase me, I stood firm. Palestine was with me, inseparable from my soul.

But the true light of that day wasn't my diploma; it was Ibrahim, my six-year-old son. His innocent smile illuminated the moment, his tiny hands clapping with pure joy, unaware of the shadows over our lives. To him, his father was simply graduating. To me, I was showing him that no force could stop me from building a future for him.

Michel Shehadeh at his graduation from CSULB, 1990

The road to this moment had been far from smooth. My academic journey wasn't just about coursework; it was about battling a government that sought to deport me, facing FBI surveillance, and defending my right to speak freely.

I had come from Palestine with a dream, to gain an education, to write, to seek truth. Yet that dream was hijacked by forces beyond my control. There were moments when it seemed impossible, but I persevered. I graduated.

In doing so, I proved to myself, my family, and my persecutors that I would not be erased.

The Unpredictability of Life
Life is unpredictable, shaped by forces we cannot control. We plan, strive, and fight, but life often moves to its own rhythm. It surprises us with victories when least expected, and burdens us with hardships when we feel strongest.

Where did my case fit into this unpredictable journey? I don't know. Perhaps it was a test, or destiny shaping me into something more. Or maybe, it was just life, chaotic, cruel, and beautiful.

With college behind me and a degree in hand, I should have felt relief, but the question of what's next loomed heavy. There was no time to savor my achievement; survival demanded urgency.

Poverty is an unyielding motivator, and with a family to support, I had no choice but to find work immediately.

The job hunt was grueling, but finally, a door opened, and I secured a position as a second manager at Thrifty (now Rite Aid). The timing was serendipitous; the company had just shifted its policy to prioritize college graduates for management roles. My degree had placed me ahead of the curve, and I was grateful for the stable employment it offered.

But deep down, a quiet discontent stirred. I hadn't spent years pursuing a degree in journalism just to abandon my dreams. I had envisioned a life in storytelling, a career that aligned with my passions. Instead, I was managing a retail store, far removed from the life I had imagined.

I was working hard, but for what? After just four months, I had earned the trust of my store manager, who told the regional manager that I was his favorite employee. The regional manager later shared this, expressing high expectations for my future. "If you stay," he said, "you will go far." But everything changed when a young, inexperienced manager was brought in to replace the retiring manager.

From the start, there was friction. The new manager seemed determined to assert his authority, and I felt his unease toward me, a tension beneath every exchange. Unlike me, he had no college degree, and under the company's new policy favoring degree holders, I sensed he saw me as a threat. His petty power moves made my position increasingly uncomfortable. I knew I couldn't stay.

During my long graveyard shifts, with the store empty and the hum of fluorescent lights, I wrestled with the question: How could I pursue a career in journalism under these circumstances? My name had been tied to the Los Angeles Eight case, branded with false accusations of terrorism. No newsroom would hire me. The dream that had motivated me seemed impossibly distant.

I had climbed a mountain, only to find an even higher one before me. Yet, despite the setbacks and doubts, one truth remained, I wasn't ready to give up.

Then, clarity came, sharp and undeniable. If no newsroom would hire me, I would create my own. The solution wasn't waiting for an opportunity; it was building one.

Determined, I made the difficult decision to quit Thrifty. Financial security was fragile, but something deep inside told me I had to take the leap. That leap led to the creation of Almiraat Newspaper, The Arab American Mirror, on October 4, 1991.

With that bold step, I reclaimed my passion for journalism and turned adversity into a foundation for something meaningful. Almiraat was a biweekly bilingual newspaper, dedicated to amplifying the voices of my community and countering the erasure of Palestinian truth.

The dream was collective. Almiraat was made possible through the investments of friends and the generosity of those who believed in the vision. Our workforce? Largely volunteers. But what we lacked in resources, we made up for in passion, resilience, and an unshakable sense of purpose.

Among those who stood with me was Brian Hudson, my

attorney and a steadfast pro-Palestinian activist, who became a dear friend.

Alongside him was Professor Sherna Gluck, my ally from CSULB and a lifelong friend. Together, they shouldered the editorial responsibilities for the English section.

On the Arabic side, Khalid Al-Sharafi and Mohammad Arid played vital roles. Khalid covered social events, capturing the essence of our community, while Mohammad managed the sports section, bringing it to life with his love for soccer. His section quickly became a favorite, captivating readers with his passion and expertise.

I eventually lost touch with Khalid, but Mohammad remained a close friend. Our bond deepened when I later married his wife's sister, Abeer, making him family.

A Voice for the Community

Almiraat resonated deeply. It wasn't just a newspaper; it was a bridge connecting Arab Americans to their heritage, struggles, and triumphs. It also reached English-speaking allies eager to understand Palestine without Western propaganda.

I poured my heart into every issue, long nights of writing, editing, and coordinating to ensure timely publication with sharp, timely analysis.

Even now, as I sift through old issues, I'm struck by the quality of the writing and the accuracy of our perspectives. We saw the patterns before they were recognized, spoke truths before they were acknowledged, and carried voices that others tried to silence.

But not everything about Almiraat was fulfilling. The business side, the endless task of selling ads, was a nightmare. Convincing Arab American small business owners to invest was like climbing a steep hill, and collecting payment was another exhausting ordeal. I later learned this struggle was shared by ethnic newspapers across the country.

Despite the financial difficulties, we scraped by. The paper paid for its office rent and covered its modest expenses, barely.

Yet, Almiraat was worth it. I was immersed in the pulse of my community, connected to its struggles and resilience. We weren't just reporting history, we were part of it. We were shaping the narrative, challenging distortions, and refusing to let Palestine's truth be buried.

Every article, every issue, was an act of resistance, a declaration that we were here and would not be silenced.

Michel Shehadeh elected President of the Arab American Press Guild (AAPG), pictured with the Guild's board and past presidents, 1995

In time, I was honored to be elected president of the Arab American Press Guild (AAPG) in 1995. This was a testament to Almiraat's standing in the community, the trust we had built, and the impact we had made.

With this role came new responsibilities, but also a renewed sense of purpose. Public service had always been my guiding force.

Almiraat was never just a newspaper; it was a movement, a testament to the power of collective voice. Telling our stories was to defy erasure, to report our truths was to stand against suppression. Holding space for our voices ensured we would not be silenced.

But just as momentum was building, the case intervened. Its shadow stretched over everything, and even this vital venture, Almiraat, couldn't escape its weight. The government's relentless pursuit and the suffocating grip of repression came crashing down again.

What happened next would test everything I had built.

The Israel Connection

On October 27, 1992, Khader and I were told our deportation trial would begin before Immigration Judge Bruce Einhorn.

By this point, we had spent five years in legal and political battles, enduring shifting accusations, delays, and an unrelenting campaign to criminalize our activism.

The government had abandoned the McCarran-Walter Act charges, replacing them with charges under the Immigration Act of 1990, accusing us of offering "material support for a terrorist organization."

The language changed, but the intent remained the same: to punish us for our beliefs, weaponize immigration law against dissent, and set a chilling precedent for activists across the U.S.

Under the new legal framework, any support for a designated "terrorist" group, whether for violence or humanitarian aid, was grounds for deportation.

It didn't matter if the aid supported orphanages, hospitals, food, or shelter. Any association, no matter how indirect, was criminalized.

Palestinians organizing fundraisers for refugees, South Africans raising money for anti-apartheid relief, and Kurds collecting donations for medical supplies were all at risk.

Humanitarianism itself was being criminalized as long as the recipients resisted oppression. This law wasn't about fighting terrorism; it was about controlling narratives and determining who could resist.

When we arrived at the Federal Building in Los Angeles for our trial, the atmosphere was heavy with intimidation.

The eighth floor had heightened security, with visitors forced through metal detectors and subjected to additional searches. The dehumanization was deliberate, eerily familiar.

I knew this kind of militarized courtroom, though not in the U.S., but in Israeli military courts, where Palestinians were tried under apartheid laws. Yet, here I was, standing in a U.S. court, in a country that claimed to uphold democracy and the rule of law, while the government sought to banish me for my political beliefs. It felt as though I had never left the occupation behind.

CHAPTER TWENTY-ONE

ROOM 8351

The Court of Bankrupt Justice

The courtroom for our hearing was labeled Room 8351, the Bankruptcy Court. The irony wasn't lost on me.

This was the bankruptcy of justice, the moral collapse of due process, where legal proceedings were designed not to protect rights but to strip them away.

This was the moment that would determine our fate: Would we be deported? Would we stay? Would this trial set a dangerous precedent for political activism in America?

The stakes were high, not just for the LA Eight, but for the entire Palestinian American community, Arab and Muslim immigrants, and activists of every background who challenged U.S. foreign policy.

If we lost, the message would be clear: "Stay silent, or risk everything." A ruling against us would shatter any illusion of free speech for immigrants in America, cementing a legal precedent where political activism could lead to deportation.

Dissent against U.S. foreign policy, especially on Palestine, would become too risky. Fear would silence voices, pushing a marginalized community further into the shadows.

This trial was about erasing the Palestinian narrative in America, ensuring no one challenged Israel's occupation, U.S. complicity, or the endless cycle of oppression.

On the day of the hearing, the weight of the moment was

undeniable.

Over a hundred organizations had urged Attorney General William Barr to drop the charges, recognizing that this case wasn't just about deportation, it was about criminalizing political expression and association in the U.S.

The courtroom wasn't just filled with prosecutors and attorneys; it was packed with witnesses to justice. Representatives from the International Commission of Jurists, National Lawyers Guild, Middle East Watch, and Amnesty International were present, fully aware of the trial's broader implications.

The government needed a spectacle, so they introduced a surprise witness: Ariel Merari, an Israeli "anti-terrorism expert" from Tel Aviv University.

Merari was a longtime advisor to the Israeli Prime Minister's office, deeply entrenched in Israel's security establishment since 1979. His price tag? $200 an hour, with expenses covered by U.S. taxpayers.

His role was clear: to label the Popular Front for the Liberation of Palestine (PFLP) as a "terrorist organization" and lay the groundwork for the U.S. government's attempt to criminalize Palestinian political activism.

Merari was not an objective witness; his job was to secure a political conviction, a narrative shaped by Israeli and U.S. interests. His history exposed his bias: He had collaborated with South Africa's Institute for Strategic Studies during apartheid, a regime notorious for its brutal repression of Black South Africans.

The connection was striking. Just as apartheid South Africa justified its crimes, Merari was now in a U.S. courtroom attempting to justify Israel's repression of Palestinians, including those like us who simply spoke out against it.

The "Captured Documents" from Israel

By the third day of the hearing, the government introduced new evidence, Israeli military "captured documents" allegedly recovered during Israel's 1982 invasion of Lebanon.

Judge Bruce Einhorn, to his credit, refused to admit them, as the government had violated the court's order requiring all evidence to be disclosed by May 15.

These documents, hastily introduced as a last-minute tactic, were empty, nothing substantial against us. But buried within them was something far more significant:

The documents confirmed what we, along with our legal and political teams, had argued for years. The Israeli and U.S. governments had worked together to orchestrate our deportation case.

The documents had been hand-delivered to the U.S. by Yigal Carmon, a senior Israeli counterterrorism official, with explicit approval from the Israeli Prime Minister in October 1990.

This wasn't about national security; it was a geopolitical maneuver, a collaboration to criminalize the Palestinian narrative in America. These documents were manufactured as weapons in a political trial, disguised as an immigration hearing.

The entire case was shaped not by evidence, but by political pressure from Israel, which viewed us as an example to intimidate Palestinians worldwide.

A Case Built on Sand

The government's prosecution had two tasks:

- Prove that the Popular Front for the Liberation of Palestine (PFLP) was a "terrorist organization" and that the Immigration and Naturalization Service (INS) had the authority to designate it as such.
- Prove that we, Khader, myself, and the LA 8, were members of the PFLP.

The first task fell to Ariel Merari, an Israeli propaganda expert. His testimony, steeped in bias, was full of vague assertions, undisclosed military intelligence sources, and broad claims that collapsed under cross-examination.

The second task, proving our membership in the PFLP, was even harder, because it wasn't true. None of us were accused of planning, participating in, or supporting any violent activities.

Our real "crime"? Political speech, humanitarian organizing, and challenging U.S. and Israeli policies. That's what they wanted to deport us for.

Desperate to strengthen their case, the government called Paul Wilkinson, a so-called terrorism expert from Aberdeen University, Scotland.

His credentials crumbled under scrutiny. He knew little about the "Middle East," the PLO, or the PFLP. He couldn't even credibly discuss the so-called "PFLP terrorist activities" chronology, which he and Merari had authored.

Instead, he relied on shallow generalizations about "patterns and trends" in terrorism, a method so flimsy that it barely held up in theory, let alone in a court of law.

Wilkinson's main role was to interpret newly declassified intelligence summaries from the CIA and other U.S. agencies, documents Judge Einhorn had forced the government to hand over after months of legal pressure.

But these reports, heavily redacted and often contradictory, failed to prove anything. Many didn't link the PFLP to specific attacks, and some even cast doubt on whether the alleged incidents had occurred at all. Not a single primary source was presented.

The so-called evidence was hearsay, recycled media reports, and unverified third-hand accounts. By the time Wilkinson finished his testimony in December 1993, his role had been an embarrassing failure.

The government spent a fortune flying in "experts" who couldn't withstand basic scrutiny. By 1992-1993, it was painfully clear that the case rested on a shaky, unproven foundation.

The chronology of alleged PFLP "attacks" was a jumbled mess, unsubstantiated by any evidence. Even Ariel Merari, the prosecution's star witness, admitted his "research" came from Israeli military intelligence, intelligence he refused to disclose or verify.

When confronted, Merari stonewalled and evaded, and Judge Einhorn could see the government's case collapsing under the weight of its own fabrication. What they called "evidence" was nothing more than a political narrative disguised as a legal case.

The Toll: A Newspaper Silenced

The hearings consumed our lives in 1992 and 1993. We were in court daily, countering baseless accusations. The personal toll was immense. With no other choice, I made the painful decision to shut down Almiraat.

The newspaper that had given our community a voice, the project that had been my lifeblood, was silenced, not by lack of passion, but by the relentless force of this case, which demanded all my energy, time, and resources.

Sadness and despair crept in, suffocating and heavy. It wasn't just disappointment, it was something deeper, something that settled into my bones.

For the first time, I questioned everything. Why had I fought so hard? Why had I sacrificed so much for a country that refused to accept me, that inflicted pain on my family, and erased everything I tried to build?

The struggle had always been exhausting, but this was different. It felt like standing at the edge of an abyss, wondering if I had the strength to continue.

I had built something meaningful, Almiraat was my voice, my resistance, proof that we existed. Losing it felt like losing part of myself, watching something precious slip through my fingers.

But it was only one sacrifice among many.

The case had stolen twenty years of my life. Two decades of legal warfare, fighting for the right to exist without being hunted, labeled, and demonized. The battle left scars that no ruling could erase.

I felt drained and hollow. For the first time, I wondered if it had all been for nothing.

Then I looked at Ibrahim, his bright eyes, his effortless laughter, his world still untouched by cynicism. In him, I saw everything I was trying to protect, everything I had fought for. He was my anchor, my reminder that my struggle wasn't just about me.

Every choice I made, every sacrifice, every piece of myself given to this fight, it was shaping his future. And in that moment, something shifted.

I remembered why I had chosen this path: to walk the path of justice, no matter how few walk it. Now, I had to expand it, no matter the cost. A lost newspaper was a small setback in a larger struggle. They could destroy, but I could rebuild. That's a Palestinian trait.

Look at Gaza, the West Bank, the refugee camps, how many times has Israel reduced our cities, homes, and dreams to rubble? And how many times have we rebuilt? We are builders. It's in our blood, in our history, in our DNA.

The sorrow still sat heavy in my chest, but I refused to let it root. Everything that had kept me fighting over the years rushed back, and I knew, the blow that doesn't break you makes you stronger.

Oslo: A Moment of Hope Turned Betrayal

Israeli Prime Minister Yitzhak Rabim, former U.S. President Bill Clinton, and Yasser Arafat at the Oslo Accords signing ceremony at the white House, 1993

The signing of the Oslo Accords on September 13, 1993, was supposed to be a turning point, when the sacrifices of the First Intifada would finally yield self-determination for Palestinians.

I remember watching the ceremony on the White House lawn, the world's eyes on the handshake between Yasser Arafat and

Yitzhak Rabin, with Bill Clinton standing between them, orchestrating history.

For many, it was a euphoric moment. Palestinians dared to hope. The streets of the West Bank and Gaza erupted in celebrations, people waving flags and singing. After decades of occupation, this was supposed to mark the dawn of Palestinian statehood.

But Oslo was not a peace treaty; it was a set of agreements that reshaped the Palestinian struggle.

What we got was not freedom. We got a rearrangement of our chains. Under Oslo, Palestinians were promised self-rule in parts of the West Bank and Gaza through the Palestinian Authority (PA).

In reality, Oslo entrenched the occupation. Illegal Israeli settlements expanded, Palestinians were denied sovereignty over borders, resources, and airspace, and the right of return for refugees was ignored. Jerusalem remained under Israeli control.

Instead of an independent state, Oslo created a subcontractor for Israel's occupation, a Palestinian Authority tasked with policing its own people.

The PLO, which had led the Palestinian resistance for decades, traded its revolutionary legitimacy for political survival. It gave up core demands in exchange for vague promises and a seat at the table.

The PLO, once the heart of the Palestinian struggle, was now reduced to an entity dependent on Israeli and American approval. It was a historic betrayal. Arafat's decision to sign the Oslo Accords split the Palestinian movement.

Some saw him as a hero, others as a leader who had compromised too much, trading the struggle for an illusion of power.

The Palestinian Authority, born from Oslo, became more

invested in its own survival than in fighting for liberation. Instead of resisting the occupation, it became its enforcer.

Oslo wasn't just a political agreement; it was a strategic shift. Before Oslo, the world saw Palestinians fighting for freedom against a brutal occupation. After Oslo, Palestinians were portrayed as partners in a failed peace process.

This shift was catastrophic, allowing Israel to frame the occupation as a conflict between two equal sides, rather than what it truly was, colonial domination.

The Israeli government used Oslo as cover to continue land grabs while pretending to negotiate peace. The world stopped seeing Israel as an occupier and started viewing it as a country in a never-ending dispute with the Palestinians.

Oslo's Impact on the L.A. 8 Case

As the Oslo Accords fractured Palestinian political unity, our case dragged on with no resolution. The U.S. government didn't abandon its efforts to deport us just because the PLO signed a peace deal.

If anything, Oslo made it easier for them to justify our persecution. They could claim that "legitimate" Palestinians were negotiating peace, while we, Palestinians in the diaspora, were "radicals" unwilling to embrace the new political reality.

But we knew the truth. The U.S. didn't want peace; it wanted submission. And we, the L.A. 8, were not willing to submit.

For a time, I held on to hope, perhaps the Palestinian leadership had a plan, perhaps Oslo would lead to something real. But in 1994, a moment shattered any illusions.

Israeli settler Baruch Goldstein walked into the Ibrahimi

Mosque in Hebron during Ramadan and opened fire, killing 29 Palestinian worshippers. He was an extremist follower of Rabbi Meir Kahane, the founder of the Jewish Defense League (JDL), responsible for the 1985 assassination of Alex Odeh in the U.S.

How did Israel respond? It imposed a curfew on Palestinian residents of Hebron, collectively punishing the victims while the settlers remained free. Instead of disarming the settlers, Israel tightened its grip on Palestinian neighborhoods and expanded settlements. Oslo had changed nothing.

The violence, land theft, and oppression continued. Oslo wasn't a path to peace; it was a trap.

In 1995, Yitzhak Rabin was assassinated by right-wing extremist Yigal Amir, who saw Rabin's peace efforts as a betrayal. This marked the beginning of the end for the Oslo Accords.

Today, the same extremist forces responsible for the Ibrahimi Mosque massacre and Rabin's assassination govern Israel, led by Benjamin Netanyahu.

By the late 1990s, it was clear that Oslo had failed. Even its most enthusiastic supporters could no longer deny reality. The Israeli government had no intention of allowing a Palestinian state. The Palestinian leadership had lost its legitimacy, and the U.S. remained fully committed to protecting Israeli apartheid.

Oslo was supposed to end the occupation, but instead, it restructured it to make it more sustainable for Israel. The Palestinian Authority was left to manage daily life under occupation, while Israel controlled the land, borders, resources, and economy. This wasn't peace; it was colonialism reinvented.

At the time, I was part of a small, dissenting minority who viewed Oslo with skepticism. The world embraced the illusion of peace, and those of us who questioned it were vilified.

We were called extremists, rejectionists, anti-peace, the same accusations the U.S. had used to justify its case against us.

The pressure to conform to the Oslo process was immense. The message was clear: Get in line, or be cast out.

But I couldn't lie to myself, I saw through the illusion. And history has vindicated us. Today, Oslo is recognized as a failure, not just by its critics, but by many who once championed it.

Instead of peace, Oslo entrenched the occupation.

Settlements expanded, Israel retained military control, and Palestinians remained stateless and powerless. The Palestinian Authority became an enforcer of Israeli security.

Oslo was not a step toward liberation; it was a mechanism for prolonged injustice, a trap that left Palestinians worse off than before. Even Rabin, Oslo's architect, was assassinated not by a Palestinian, but by an Israeli right-wing extremist, the kind that now dominates Israel's government under Netanyahu.

Oslo was never meant to be honored; it was designed to neutralize Palestinian resistance while Israel consolidated its grip on the land.

I will never forget a picnic organized by my town's Birzeit Association in Southern California. It felt like home, the aroma of grilled lamb, Dabkeh dancing, and warm laughter.

But the conversation inevitably turned to Oslo. I tried to explain why it was a dangerous deception, pointing out the lack of clarity and Israel's continued control over everything important. I warned that it wasn't liberation, it was a trap.

But the mood was optimistic. They wanted to believe. One man, frustrated by my skepticism, asked, "Why is it whenever we get close to peace, you reject it?" Many around us nodded in agreement.

I understood why they wanted to believe. Palestinians had endured decades of dispossession, exile, and occupation; any hope felt irresistible. For many, Oslo felt like the closest we had come to reclaiming our homeland.

But I had seen too much to be swept away by hope alone. Those of us who opposed it were labeled radicals, accused of preferring war over peace, when in reality, we refused to accept the illusion of freedom.

Oslo did exactly what it was meant to do: It bought time for Israel, neutralized international pressure, divided the Palestinian movement, and co-opted Palestinian leadership into managing the occupation.

It wasn't a step toward statehood; it was a strategy to ensure we never achieved it. We were right to oppose it.

Back then, our warnings were dismissed. Now, the truth is undeniable. Oslo has failed. Even its strongest defenders can't argue otherwise.

We were right to say that Palestine will not be liberated through empty agreements dictated by its oppressors, but through the unwavering struggle of its people.

Palestinians didn't fight for decades just to end up with a self-governing prison. We didn't endure exile, massacres, and occupation just to settle for less than justice, freedom, and our full rights.

Liberation cannot be negotiated with the colonizer; it must be won. Palestine will be free, not because of Oslo, but despite it.

Chapter Twenty-One

Arafat's Fall and the Rise of Submission

Arafat had been cornered, forced to surrender to Israel's vision, dressed as a pathway to peace. The signs were clear from the beginning, but many were blinded by the allure of hope, unable to see the trap.

Oslo didn't just betray the Palestinian cause; it led to Arafat's political demise and, as many believe, his assassination through Israeli poisoning. His fall marked the end of an era, and in his place rose Mahmoud Abbas, whose rule became synonymous with submission, corruption, and complicity.

Under Abbas, the Palestinian Authority (PA) became a security subcontractor for Israel. Instead of mobilizing for liberation, Abbas pursued pacification, repression, and division. The PA prioritized its own survival over the liberation of its people, undermining Palestinian resistance.

The Erosion of Palestinian Activism in the U.S.

Oslo didn't just fracture Palestinian resistance at home; it dealt a devastating blow to activism in the U.S.

For decades, we had worked tirelessly to mobilize students and forge alliances with Black, Latino, and Asian communities. Through relentless organizing, we made Palestinian rights a core civil liberties issue. For the first time, Palestinian rights were championed by Palestinians themselves.

But piece by piece, the movement began to unravel. Not dramatically, but gradually. Through surveillance, repression, and political pressure, Zionist forces became more coordinated and aggressive. They didn't erase our victories overnight, but they weakened them step by step.

Even in academia, where we had secured victories advocating for Palestinian academic freedom, our influence began to fade.

Public support eroded as the opposition adapted and intensified its attacks.

Oslo's betrayal wasn't just in its failed promises; it was in the deliberate destruction of grassroots activism, both in Palestine and abroad.

Instead of nurturing the Palestinian movement, the PA dismantled it. In the U.S., where Palestinian organizing had flourished independently for decades, the PA's weak offices replaced the vibrant activism that once defined our struggle.

Where there had been mobilization, there was now stagnation. Where there had been confrontation of Zionism, there was now timid diplomacy. Where there had been independent leadership, there was now PA-sponsored suppression.

Rather than uniting Palestinians, the PA became a tool of control, ensuring that Palestinian voices in the diaspora remained fragmented and ineffective. It wasn't just incompetence; it was an abandonment of the Palestinian struggle for liberation.

By the mid-1990s, Palestinian activism in the U.S. was in crisis. Many institutions we had built collapsed or faded into irrelevance. One of the greatest losses was the General Union of Palestine Students (GUPS).

Once a powerful force with chapters across major universities, GUPS had led protests, built alliances, and made Palestine central to progressive politics. Then, it began to wither.

The decline was not accidental. With Oslo, the PA's interference, and increasing surveillance, the Palestinian voice in America was weakened. The void left behind was filled by broader Arab American activism, but the unique Palestinian presence faded.

It was a painful reversal, the unraveling of years of effort. Yet, nothing built with passion ever truly disappears. There were times it felt all was lost, that new generations were disconnected, but history remembers, and history doesn't remain buried forever.

CHAPTER TWENTY-TWO

FROM FEAR TO ADVOCACY

The Arab American Response to Domestic Terrorism

On the afternoon of April 19, 1995, while navigating Los Angeles' highways, I heard the breaking news: A massive car bomb exploded at the Alfred P. Murrah Federal Building in Oklahoma City, killing 168 people, including nineteen children, and injuring over five hundred.

My heart raced. A wave of dread crashed over me. I knew what was coming.

The inevitable backlash. The blind rage. The accusations. If the perpetrators were Arabs or Muslims, we, Arab and Muslim communities, would be blamed before the facts were even known.

The headlines confirmed my fears. News anchors speculated about "Middle Eastern extremists." Sketches of "Arab suspects" flashed on the screen. Anonymous sources talked about "terrorist networks." The narrative was set before a single fact had been established.

The panic within our community was immediate. We prepared for the harassment we knew would come, drafting "Know Your Rights" materials, preparing for FBI visits, and reminding people to protect themselves legally.

For two hours, every Arab and Muslim in America felt hunted. The fear was palpable in every phone call, every uneasy interaction, every glance.

Then, the truth emerged.

Timothy McVeigh, an American, was arrested in connection with the bombing. A white man, a Gulf War veteran, not an Arab, not a Muslim. The "Middle Eastern terrorists" had never existed. The media hysteria, the whispers, and the suspicions, were all lies.

McVeigh, wearing a T-shirt with an image of Abraham Lincoln and the phrase "sic semper tyrannis," was a homegrown terrorist.

The moment his identity was revealed, the media's tone softened. They debated his "disillusionment with the government" and discussed his "personal grievances." If McVeigh had been Palestinian or Muslim, the reaction would have been different; there would have been no introspection, just blame.

America does not define terrorism by the act itself, but by who commits it. For two hours, we were all guilty. Then, just as quickly, the fear and racial profiling disappeared.

As I sat with my family that night, watching the news, anger welled up inside me, anger that words could hardly capture.

They had wanted it to be us. They had needed it to be us. The system was primed, the headlines pre-written, and the enemy chosen before the crime was even solved. That was the most terrifying realization.

Five years after the attack, in 2000, President Clinton stood before the wreckage of the Alfred P. Murrah Federal Building. A memorial had been erected, 168 empty chairs, each representing a life lost in the attack. Some were small, marking the children who perished.

The memorial was meant to symbolize remembrance and resilience, but for many, the scars never faded. The Oklahoma City bombing wasn't just an attack on a building; it was an assault on the American psyche, shattering the illusion that terrorism was always foreign, always had a different face, name, or god. McVeigh was a product of America itself, its militarism, anti-government fervor, and white nationalist extremism.

Yet, despite the magnitude of his crime, no war was declared on white militias, no policies to surveil angry young white men, no calls to detain thousands without charge. McVeigh's face didn't fit the narrative of terror.

For two hours, the entire Arab and Muslim community was held responsible for a crime we didn't commit. Then, as quickly as the suspicion appeared, it disappeared, without apology, acknowledgment, or justice.

The hypocrisy, like the bombing itself, left a crater that could never be filled.

Building an Arab American Political Agenda

The Oklahoma bombing forced our community to confront a critical question: How do we navigate life in America under these conditions?

I found myself at the heart of a shift in Arab American advocacy, steering through a transformation, one that was strategic but unsettling. The Palestinian-led grassroots movement that once defined Arab American activism was retreating, giving way to a new model focused on institutionalized political engagement.

Where we once relied on mass mobilization, there was now a growing push to integrate Arab American voices into U.S. political power. The key question was: Could Palestine remain central to the Arab American political agenda in this new, constrained environment?

In 1996, as president of the Arab American Press Guild (AAPG), I organized the seminar "Toward an Arab American

Agenda," aimed at examining how we could advocate for Arab American rights while keeping Palestine central to the movement.

Among the speakers were influential figures in Arab American political life:

- Dr. Hala Salam Maksoud from the Arab American University Graduates (AAUG), the oldest Arab American organization, a powerhouse of intellectual and political thought.
- Mr. Hamza Al Mughrabi, president of the American-Arab Anti-Discrimination Committee (ADC), focused on fighting discrimination and defending Arab identity.
- Mr. Khalil Jahshan, president of the National Association of Arab Americans (NAAA), pushing for Arab American political representation.
- And I, as president of the AAPG, representing the Arab American media and its role in shaping political discourse.

A Shift in Strategy

The shift from grassroots activism to policy engagement was strategic but came at a cost. The raw passion of direct action and mass mobilization began to dilute in the slow, bureaucratic processes of lobbying and electoral politics.

We had entered a new phase, one offering political leverage but also constraints of compromise and institutional limitations. The Palestinian cause was no longer shouted in the streets; it was now negotiated in boardrooms and policy discussions. Both approaches, I realized, were necessary.

Even as institutional organizations led advocacy, the responsibility of keeping the Palestinian cause alive beyond political talking points remained with us, the community, activists, journalists, and storytellers. Without a strong grassroots movement, Palestine risked becoming just another agenda item, rather than the urgent cause it truly is.

My first major event as president of the Arab American Press Guild (AAPG), "Toward an Arab American Agenda," was a resounding success. Over 250 attendees from more than 40 Arab American organizations signaled a new era of political engagement. It was a significant step forward for AAPG, expanding it into a national platform.

A Night of Conversation and New Beginnings

The next day, I invited Dr. Hala Salam Maksoud to dinner with AAPG board members. After the event, we had a deep conversation about the evolving needs of the Arab American community and the movement's future.

Michel Shehadeh with the late Dr. Hala Salam Maksoud, National President of the American-Arab Anti-Discrimination Committee (ADC)

I had long admired Dr. Maksoud for her strategic brilliance and unyielding commitment to justice. Our visions aligned, deepening my respect for her. That evening wasn't just a dinner; it was a turning point.

Later that year, Dr. Maksoud, now national president of the American-Arab Anti-Discrimination Committee (ADC), offered me the role of Western Regional Director, the same position once held by Alex Odeh, a Palestinian-American civil rights leader assassinated by the Jewish Defense League (JDL) in 1985.

Taking this role meant stepping into a legacy of sacrifice, carrying forward a mission that had been targeted for destruction. It was more than a job; it was a calling, a chance to continue fighting for Arab American rights, civil liberties, and justice for Palestine.

That same year, I earned my master's degree in public administration from CSULB. Everything, my education, experiences, and activism, had led to this moment. I accepted the offer, stepping into a new chapter that demanded resilience, courage, and unwavering commitment to justice.

A New Vision, A New Challenge

At the time, the ADC was struggling, teetering on the edge of collapse due to financial and political pressures. Dr. Maksoud stepped in when no one else would. She was determined to rebuild the ADC with a renewed sense of purpose. Her vision was clear: the ADC would be independent and accountable only to the community.

When she hired me, she told me, "I'm hiring you not as a manager, but as a political ally to help rebuild the ADC. If the community can't sustain the organization, then they don't deserve it." This principle was non-negotiable: The ADC would not take money from Arab regimes. It would stand independent, without political compromise. This resonated with my beliefs, cementing my commitment to the role.

Under Dr. Maksoud's leadership, we weren't just reviving an organization, we were rebuilding a movement with Palestine at its heart.

The Day the World Changed

Since my hiring at ADC, my time was consumed by Arab American advocacy. I tackled issues like negative Arab stereotyping in pop culture, racism, lobbying, the L.A. 8 case, and, of course, Palestine.

On September 11, 2001, I was sitting at my kitchen table when the first plane struck the Twin Towers. As I watched in horror, I knew what was coming. Arabs and Muslims in America would be blamed.

For years, we had been fighting for justice in Palestine and standing against U.S. foreign policy. But 9/11 was different. The media named the hijackers, Arab, Muslim, and our community became a target.

I had already spent years under government harassment as one of the Los Angeles Eight, trapped in a Kafkaesque legal battle. But after 9/11, the government's repression reached a new level.

As the Western Regional Director of the ADC, I was responsible for defending the civil rights of Arab Americans. That morning, I felt it in my bones, mass arrests, racial profiling, and a new wave of surveillance were imminent.

We had already battled decades of negative stereotyping and Islamophobia, but now the full force of state repression and public hostility was descending on our communities. Overnight, Arabs and Muslims in America became suspects.

A Nation in Fear, A Community Under Siege

The PATRIOT Act expanded surveillance powers, making mosques, community centers, and activist organizations targets for infiltration. The FBI intensified its efforts to silence voices advocating for Palestine. "Terrorism" was weaponized, equating Arabs, Muslims, and resistance to the American empire with extremism.

Thousands of Arab and Muslim men were detained, many

without charge. Families were torn apart, and communities lived in constant fear of government action. The media fed the hysteria, portraying Arabs and Muslims as threats.

Hate crimes surged. Mosques were vandalized, businesses attacked, and hijab-wearing women assaulted. In the wake of 9/11, the message was clear: being Arab or Muslim meant living under suspicion.

I spent my days fielding calls from terrified community members, organizing legal support, and meeting with civil rights groups. I tried, against the tide of fear and repression, to remind America that we, too, grieved, that our rights mattered. But the machinery of war had already been set in motion.

The War on Terror: A Global Crusade

9/11 set the stage for the U.S.'s most destructive wars of the 21st century. The invasion of Afghanistan was justified as retaliation against al-Qaeda and the Taliban. Then came Iraq in 2003, built on lies about weapons of mass destruction and Saddam Hussein's alleged ties to terrorism.

These wars killed hundreds of thousands, displaced millions, and entrenched American military dominance, reinforcing the false notion of a civilizational war against Islam. Guantanamo Bay, Abu Ghraib, drone assassinations, and secret renditions became the hallmarks of America's new, lawless war.

The War on Terror wasn't just about hunting down the perpetrators of 9/11; it was about reshaping the world in America's image, imposing its will through force, and ensuring its empire's dominance.

And Palestine was always part of this equation. As the U.S. waged wars in Afghanistan and Iraq, Israel used the moment to further its colonial project, branding Palestinian resistance as "terrorism" and deepening its military occupation with full U.S. support.

Israel capitalized on 9/11, portraying itself as a victim of Islamic extremism, equating Palestinian resistance with al-Qaeda, and using global hysteria to justify its repression of the Second Intifada. The rhetoric of the War on Terror became a gift to Zionism, with Israeli leaders adopting the language of "security" to justify atrocities.

The U.S. adopted Israeli tactics, militarized policing, mass surveillance, and indefinite detention, under the guise of "national security." Both systems of oppression reinforced the narrative that Arabs and Muslims were the enemy, and their resistance, whether in Gaza, Iraq, Kabul, or New York, was terrorism.

Despite the fear and repression, I saw resilience. A new generation of Arab and Muslim activists emerged, refusing to be silenced and organizing against the surveillance state, racism, and Islamophobia gripping the nation.

We marched against the wars, built coalitions, and demanded justice, not just for our communities but for all those shattered by the American empire. Despite years of war, injustice, and suffering, one truth remains: we are still here, still fighting.

Any resistance to Israeli occupation, whether armed, unarmed, political, or humanitarian, was framed as "terrorism." This shifted global discourse, allowing Israel to escalate its military campaigns under the guise of its own "War on Terror," a narrative embraced by the U.S. without hesitation.

Aid to Israel surged, diplomatic cover was granted for massacres, and the U.S. provided ideological support for a more brutal occupation. While American bombs fell on Afghanistan and Iraq, Israeli tanks rolled through Palestinian cities with renewed impunity. The message was clear: Palestine was one of the War on

Chapter Twenty-Two

Terror's first battlegrounds.

Inside the U.S., 9/11 fractured Arab and Muslim communities. Some distanced themselves from political engagement to avoid becoming targets. But many, like us, refused silence. We refused to cower, to accept the criminalization of our existence.

If the Oklahoma bombing had tortured our community, 9/11 was a living hell. The perpetrators were Arab and Muslim, and the backlash was unprecedented. The entire U.S. security apparatus and media machine mobilized to cast us as the enemy.

Every racist stereotype was unleashed. We were painted as Saddam Hussein, Osama bin Laden, and the Taliban. From TV programs to Hollywood scripts, we became the villainous "other."

Mosques were vandalized. Arabs and Muslims were attacked. Sikh men were murdered for wearing turbans. Muslim women in hijabs were assaulted. Our children were bullied, and our businesses targeted. The American flag became a symbol of hostility, marking anyone who looked like us as a suspect.

Then came the detentions. Thousands of Arab and Muslim men were rounded up, held without charge, interrogated, and disappeared. Families were torn apart. Green card holders and visa applicants had their futures stolen in an instant.

While we grieved the innocent lives lost in New York and Washington, we were told we had no right to grieve. We had to prove our innocence, apologize for crimes we didn't commit. 9/11 cemented the next phase of American imperialism, a permanent state of endless war, normalized surveillance, indefinite detention, and racial profiling.

The full weight of U.S. military might was deployed not for justice but to expand the empire. Torture sites like Abu Ghraib and

Guantanamo Bay became symbols of moral collapse. Drone wars escalated, terrorizing villages in Pakistan, Yemen, and Somalia.

Meanwhile, Israel watched and learned. The walls of the West Bank grew taller. Settlements expanded. Checkpoints multiplied. Gaza became more suffocating, with every Israeli soldier's action justified as "security."

The language of the War on Terror merged with Zionism, and Palestine became a forgotten battlefield in America's global war. Despite the repression and fear of the post-9/11 world, we refused to disappear. If anything, we grew louder.

As the U.S. waged war abroad and turned its security state inward, the anti-war movement grew. Activists, especially young people, began to see the connections between U.S. militarism and the erosion of civil liberties at home.

The struggle for Palestinian rights continued, even as the risks of speaking out increased. The truth of the American empire became undeniable, and cracks in its hegemony started to show.

For me, 9/11 was a defining moment, but not in the way American politicians framed it. It wasn't an attack on "freedom" or "values." It was the result of decades of U.S. foreign policy, destabilizing regions, supporting dictators, and waging war under the guise of democracy.

It marked the beginning of a new era of struggle, where we, Palestinians, Arabs, and American advocates for justice, had to be bolder than ever.

CHAPTER TWENTY-THREE

MARKED BEFORE THE CRIME
Living Arab in Post-9/11 America

Racism often strikes without warning, suddenly, in a moment that leaves you stunned, questioning how a stranger can see in you the embodiment of everything they despise.

One such moment occurred while visiting my friend Hikmat in Phoenix. We were strolling through a mall, enjoying the cool air conditioning to escape the desert heat.

Out of nowhere, a large man stepped into my path. At first, I thought it was an accident, but his hostile glare quickly showed otherwise. Without a word, he spat out: "Tell your friend Saddam we're going to kick his ass." Before I could react, he turned and walked away.

The hatred in his eyes was unmistakable, as was his certainty that I, a total stranger, was somehow connected to Saddam Hussein simply because of how I looked. His twisted pronunciation of "Saddam," like a biblical curse, made it clear, this wasn't just an insult, but a condemnation.

I've never understood what drives such hate, to approach a stranger and lash out unprovoked. But in that moment, I realized this was a shadow of the violence others had endured. Some had paid with their lives.

Four days after 9/11, Balbir Singh Sodhi, a Sikh American, was killed in Mesa, Arizona, by Frank Roque, who targeted him for being a "raghead" he blamed for the attacks. Waqar Hasan, a Pakistani immigrant, was murdered by Mark Anthony Stroman in Dallas,

Texas, and the same man killed Vasudev Patel, an Indian American, in Mesquite, Texas. None of these victims were Arab, Muslim, or involved in 9/11; they were murdered for their appearance, targeted by those who needed a scapegoat.

This is the cost of ignorance, paid in fear, blood, and stolen lives. The demonization of Arab leaders spread across the media, infiltrating homes and classrooms. Children felt ashamed of their fathers, as the message was clear: Arab meant enemy, Arab meant bad.

How could we explain to our children that in this country, our names, faces, and heritage had become symbols of fear?

How do you protect a child from a world that sees his identity as a crime? These moments, whether a racist in a mall, a child bullied in school, or innocent men murdered for existing, are not isolated. They are symptoms of a deeper issue, fueled by decades of dehumanization, political rhetoric that fosters fear, and media narratives that reduce us to one-dimensional villains.

We saw it before 9/11. It worsened after 9/11. And it continues today, whenever an Arab, Muslim, or anyone perceived as "Middle Eastern" is treated as an outsider, a threat.

It would be easy to feel angry, exhausted, or disillusioned. But if there's one truth that has carried me through the darkest times, it's this: Our existence is resistance. Every time we refuse to bow our heads, every time we push back, we remind the world we belong. We are winning.

A Battle for Principles

After Dr. Hala Salam Maksoud's passing in 2002, the ADC lost its principled independence, becoming a tool of partisan politics. Under new leadership, the ADC, once a fearless voice against U.S. foreign policy in the "Middle East," began seeking approval from politicians and pro-Israel organizations, ignoring the repression of Arab Americans.

I clashed with the new leadership from the start. Their disregard for grassroots chapters and outreach to Zionist groups signaled a betrayal of the organization's mission. Post-9/11, the ADC caved to government pressure, promoting "cooperation" with the FBI instead of defending our community from surveillance and profiling.

By June 2002, my dissent had become intolerable to the ADC national leadership. In August, I was dismissed, not for any misconduct, but for refusing to conform to a political discourse that had abandoned its founding principles. My termination ignited national outrage. ADC chapters and longtime allies rose in protest, demanding accountability, transparency, and a return to the organization's original mission of defending civil rights with integrity and courage.

The national leadership ignored them, and the ADC lost its strongest chapters, especially in the Western region, where all twelve active branches vanished. Even as my deportation case loomed, it wasn't the U.S. government that erased me; it was ADC's national leadership. The very organization meant to protect our community aided its suppression.

History is clear. Movements for justice aren't built on institutions or titles, but on conviction. The ADC, once fearless under Dr. Maksoud, became a shadow of itself. Yet I have no regrets. Justice doesn't live in institutions alone. It lives in the streets, protests, and the new generation carrying the torch. If we don't stand for our principles, then what are we fighting for?

CHAPTER TWENTY-FOUR

AIAD'S CASE
A Fight for Justice

In late 2006, living in Bend, Oregon, I received a call from Aiad Barakat. His voice carried years of frustration, of legal limbo and bureaucratic stonewalling. Aiad wanted to sue the U.S. government for failing to comply with U.S. District Judge Stephen V. Wilson's ruling, which had granted him U.S. citizenship on June 23, 2006.

Aiad had been a legal U.S. resident since 1997, yet the government refused to honor the ruling. His life had been stuck in limbo, his business tangled in legal issues. After waiting too long, he was ready to fight back.

Aiad and I shared a deep bond, more than friendship, brotherhood forged in struggle. We had confided in each other through personal and political storms. Now, he turned to me, torn between the risks and the necessity of action. Our attorneys warned that suing the government might bring unintended consequences, not just for him but for all of us. The case against him was built on the same flimsy charges used against Khader and me.

Though those charges had been reduced to visa violations, there was always the danger of unforeseen repercussions. Still, Aiad couldn't wait any longer. After hours of deliberation, I supported his decision to sue.

December 2006 marked a pivotal moment. For two decades, the battle had been fought in legal filings, behind closed courtroom doors. None of us had ever taken the stand. Now, we had a chance to force the government to reveal the "evidence" it used to justify its persecution.

On the first day, David Cole, Aiad's lead attorney, dismantled the government's case. His calm voice painted Aiad as a man of resilience, a father, a contributor to society, a worker overseeing construction projects, who sought citizenship to vote, gain First Amendment protections, and visit his sick mother. Aiad's story was not one of a threat, but of family and contribution. But the government was determined to prove otherwise.

By the third day, the government's desperation showed. They presented years of surveillance, wiretaps, and undercover video footage. But they had no crime, no wrongdoing, and no damning evidence. Their case was empty, full of noise but devoid of substance.

Judge Wilson saw through it. His ruling was swift and scathing: "You're shooting blanks. Zero plus zero equals zero." The case collapsed.

In the end, justice prevailed. Aiad won, ending decades of persecution. His victory was personal and historic. "I've waited for this day for almost 20 years," he said, hopeful the government would quickly issue him a passport to visit his elderly mother, something he hadn't been able to do since arriving in the U.S.

David Cole, reflecting on the ruling, called it "a landmark decision," affirming that the government cannot deny citizenship based on First Amendment-protected activity.

Marc Van Der Hout of the National Lawyers Guild added, "We hope the government will not waste more resources appealing this important decision. This misguided prosecution has gone on long enough."

With the ruling, Aiad became the first of the L.A. 8 to gain U.S. citizenship.

On December 20, 2006, in a quiet but symbolic ceremony in Los Angeles, Aiad was sworn in as an American citizen, a moment that once seemed impossible. The ceremony was not just a formality; it was a triumph over oppression, a victory after years of legal battles, government attacks, and unwavering resistance.

Aiad was joined by close friends and attorneys, witnesses to a victory earned through perseverance. U.S. District Judge Dickran Tevrizian administered the Oath of Citizenship, offering his well wishes as Aiad completed his journey, shaped by resilience and the pursuit of justice.

This moment was more than a certificate; it symbolized survival, the right to belong, and the hard-fought battle won.

Aiad Barakat with L.A. Eight attorney Ahilan Arulanantham

Ahilan Arulanantham, a lawyer with the ACLU of Southern California, who worked on the L.A. 8 case, stood by Aiad. After the ceremony, Aiad asked the question that had defined our struggle for years: "What's next?"

For years, every legal proceeding ended with that question, but Ahilan's response was different: "There is no next time. This is it." For the first time, there was no new battle, no appeal, just victory.

Carol Sobel of the National Lawyers Guild expressed hope that this ruling would push the government to reconsider the cases of the remaining L.A. 8 members, granting them the justice they had long been denied.

Aiad's case was more than a legal victory. It marked a turning point, a crack in the wall of repression that had stood for twenty years. Supporting Aiad had been a risk, but his victory was one for all of us, a political witch hunt unraveling at last. For the first time in years, we felt something we had been denied: hope.

And then, we triumphed.

A Historic Rebuke, A Hard-Fought Victory
In a moment both surreal and long overdue, Immigration Judge Bruce Einhorn delivered a ruling that ended the government's two-decade-long pursuit of our deportation. He ordered the proceedings against Khader and me to be terminated. The government's case had collapsed, not due to a technicality, but because it had been flawed from the start. The truth had always been on our side.

For twenty years, the government used its power, surveillance, intimidation, and secrecy to try to break us. They had failed, and now their failure was exposed for all to see.

Judge Einhorn's words were a scathing indictment of the government's actions. He ruled that they had repeatedly withheld evidence favorable to us, violating due process, and called their actions "an embarrassment to the rule of law."

We had won. Not just for ourselves, but for every immigrant, every activist, and anyone who had been targeted for speaking truth to power.

Ahilan Arulanantham of the ACLU of Southern California, one of our attorneys, said: "The message is clear: the government should focus on real threats, not law-abiding immigrants who've done nothing wrong."

The government had failed over four presidencies. Their accusations had collapsed under scrutiny. Their secret evidence was exposed as fraudulent, and their tactics, framing political dissent as a national security threat, were laid bare as political repression.

Marc Van Der Hout of the National Lawyers Guild added, "The decision makes clear the government cannot refuse to comply with an immigration judge's orders and cannot deport permanent residents who did nothing but advocate for Palestinians' rights."

In his ruling, Judge Einhorn condemned the prolonged deportation proceedings as a "festering wound" on justice. He denounced the government's failure to uphold due process, stating it had kept us in legal limbo while being unprepared to prosecute its case.

David Cole of Georgetown Law School, who had represented us, summarized the absurdity: "For 20 years, the government tried to deport us for activities protected if we were U.S. citizens. We hope they'll focus on real terrorists now, not political activists."

And just like that, in 2007, the case that had defined my life for two decades was over.

Michel Shehadeh, with his son Ibrahim, Bashar Amer, Ayman Obeid, Aiad Barakat, and Khader Hamideh, alongside attorneys David Cole, Paul Hofman, Marc Van Der Hout, and Carol Sobel, in front of the 9th Circuit Court

Twenty years of uncertainty. Twenty years of being treated as a threat. Twenty years of our lives stolen. By the time the case concluded in 2007, the world had changed beyond recognition.

We had lived through the collapse of the Soviet Union, the invasions of Iraq and Afghanistan, two Palestinian Intifadas, and the 9/11 attacks. Each of these events profoundly shaped the American political landscape, and the justification for the U.S. government's persecution of immigrants, Arabs, and Muslims.

The war on Palestinian activism morphed into the War on Terror. The fear-mongering tactics, and propaganda remained the same, just with a different label.

Though the wounds of those twenty years will never fully heal, our victory proved that persistence, solidarity, and an unyielding belief in justice can prevail.

When the case ended, the emotions were overwhelming, relief, triumph, and grief for the years stolen from us. Relief because, for the first time in two decades, we were free. Free from uncertainty, from the constant fear of being torn from our families, free to dream and plan again.

Triumph because we stood firm, refused to break, and won. The government had thrown everything at us, surveillance, propaganda, and legal maneuvering. But knowing that justice can be achieved through persistence was exhilarating.

Yet, the victory had a bitter edge. Twenty of the best years of our lives were taken. All the achievements we could have pursued, the milestones we could have reached, the simple joys of uninterrupted living, gone.

It took nine years to have my second son, Rami, in 1992. The weight of the case robbed me of the dream of a larger family. Time slipped away, not just for me, but for my loved ones. Time lost can never be reclaimed.

Yet, through it all, I wasn't bitter or angry. I made peace with my destiny and found a greater purpose in the struggle.

CHAPTER TWENTY-FIVE

ROOTS IN STRUGGLE, BRANCHES IN HOPE
The Unfinished Fight

The case became a lesson to my children about standing up for their rights, defending the Constitution, and walking the path of justice, even when it's lonely.

I refused to let this case define me as a victim. Instead, I saw it as our contribution to the larger struggle for Palestine, a fight that continues, in far harsher conditions than we endured. Whatever suffering we faced, it paled in comparison to what Palestinians endure daily.

And despite everything, we thrived. I am grateful for my children, their success, and the mark they are leaving on this world. For my grandchildren, who bring me immeasurable joy. For love, family, and the garden that now blooms in Oregon, marking a new chapter of peace.

I'm also grateful to the courageous seven comrades who persevered. They have my love and admiration, and I wish them health, prosperity, and happiness.

The case didn't just leave scars; it became a source of inspiration. To our community, our friends, our legal team, and most of all, to the warriors of justice who stood unwaveringly beside us through every battle. To them, I owe my deepest love and thanks.

They know who they are. Their solidarity carried us through the darkest times, and for that, I'll be forever grateful.

A New Chapter: The Power of Storytelling

In 2008, I became the Executive Director of the Arab Film Festival in San Francisco. It was a dream job, a chance to combat negative stereotypes through film, instead of legal battles or political debates.

Arabs had long been vilified on the big screen, reduced to terrorists or villains. The Arab Film Festival was a platform to reclaim those narratives, showcasing love, resistance, culture, and humanity.

Under my leadership, the festival grew into one of the largest Arab film festivals outside the Arab world. It was a labor of love, driven by the belief that representation matters, that every story was an act of resistance.

Yet, as fulfilling as this work was, the distance was hard. My family remained in Bend, Oregon, while I worked in San Francisco. I missed the warmth of my children's embrace and the simple comfort of being home.

In 2013, after five incredible years, I made the difficult decision to return to my family. The time apart strained my marriage, and though we fought to hold on, some distances can't be bridged.

In 2017, my wife and I mutually decided to divorce. It wasn't bitter, but a transition, from partners to friends, and later, to grandparents. We remained deeply connected through our love for our children and grandchildren, shaped by the years we shared and the family we built.

Life is a series of beginnings and endings, and sometimes, endings lead to new beginnings.

Love, Reimagined

In 2021, love found me again. I remarried Abeer, a Palestinian American woman who brought love, understanding, and renewed joy into my life. Together, we created a home filled with warmth, where family remains at the center.

Michel Shehadeh and his wife, Abeer Shehadeh, in Oregon in 2021, where they both reside today

My children, grandchildren, Abeer, and I have built a new chapter, one that honors the past while embracing the future with hope, love, and resilience. In the end, it's not the battles that define us, but the love we hold, the family we cherish, and the stories we pass on.

The case is over, but the fire that ignited it still burns. The Palestinian people have yet to taste freedom, and the Israeli occupation has only worsened, becoming more brutal and genocidal.

In Gaza, by 2023, an Israeli campaign of annihilation had left nearly 67,000 martyrs and more than 169,000 injured among a population of approximately 2.2 million, the overwhelming majority of whom were women and children.

Israel has dropped the equivalent of six Hiroshima bombs on a 186-square-mile strip of land housing two million people. This wasn't just war. It was extermination, carried out with American weapons and money.

Now, the West Bank faces the same violence. The scale has grown, but just as we won our case, the Palestinian people will win. For decades, Zionist forces have tried to break the Palestinian spirit through massacres, displacement, imprisonment, and ethnic cleansing. But Palestinians have never wavered in their fight for their rights. They will win, because justice always prevails.

History shows us that no empire, colonizer, or occupier can defeat a people who refuse to submit. South Africa, Algeria, Vietnam, and Cuba each overcame overwhelming odds. Palestine will be no different. Liberation is inevitable. When that day comes, the world will know: the Palestinian people were always on the right side of history.

In 2023, the world saw an unprecedented global movement for Gaza. As Israel waged its war, millions took to the streets, from New York to London, from Johannesburg to Jakarta, from Buenos Aires to Berlin. Palestine was everywhere. Voices once silenced now roared across the globe. This was the culmination of decades of groundwork, blossoming when the world needed it most.

History resurfaces. Even when progress seems frozen, when movements appear defeated, their legacy endures, waiting for the right moment to awaken.

The Gaza solidarity movement of 2023 proved what we always knew: our struggle was never in vain. Despite setbacks, betrayals, and relentless attacks, the spirit of resistance is eternal. Oppression has an expiration date. As long as Palestinians exist, the struggle will continue, until Palestine is free.

Same Tactics, Trump Era: The U.S. War on Palestinian Voices

The L.A.8 case, the Mahmoud Khalil case, and others share common themes of political repression and the targeting of Palestinian activism. The U.S. government has systematically criminalized Palestinian advocacy, using vague allegations and secret evidence to justify deportation.

We were accused under McCarthy-era laws for alleged support of the PFLP, despite no criminal charges. Mahmoud Khalil faces deportation under post-9/11 laws that criminalize humanitarian aid, political speech, and solidarity with Palestinian resistance. Both cases weaponized immigration laws to silence activism and shield Israel from accountability.

A New Generation of Resistance

Mahmoud Khalil is not alone. He is part of a historic pro-Palestinian movement that has emerged across generations in response to Israel's war on Gaza. Since October 7, 2023, Israel's assault on Gaza has killed tens of thousands and displaced nearly 2 million people, with full U.S. backing. Instead of silencing the world, Israel's brutality sparked global resistance.

Students from campuses like Columbia, UCLA, and Harvard have organized protests, walkouts, and sit-ins, challenging government complicity in genocide. They've faced arrests and threats, but they continue. Mahmoud Khalil, a leader of this movement, now faces legal threats for refusing to be silenced.

The legal and political landscape has shifted dramatically since our case. Mahmoud Khalil is targeted in the repressive post-9/11 era, where terrorism laws give the U.S. unchecked power to detain and deport without due process. Under Trump, the crackdown on Palestinian advocacy is aggressive, with activists facing firings, suspensions, and violent repression.

Despite this, the solidarity movement continues to grow. It's no longer just Palestinians fighting for Palestine; it's a global front. Allies from Black Lives Matter, Indigenous sovereignty, Jewish anti-Zionists, and more stand against U.S.-Israeli imperialism. Israel's actions in Gaza and the West Bank can no longer be hidden. The global resistance proves that the struggle for Palestine is a human struggle.

A Historic Test

These cases highlight the decline of U.S. hegemony. We were targeted when American imperialism was largely unchallenged. Mahmoud Khalil, however, fights in an era where Palestinian resistance is stronger, and U.S. influence is waning amid global shifts.

Our case proved that legal resistance, community mobilization, and public pressure could force the U.S. to retreat from political persecution. Khalil's case is a test of whether Palestinian voices can continue to break through repression, challenge the U.S. crackdown, and remain steadfast in the fight for justice.

His case is ours. His struggle is ours. His freedom is ours. As long as there is injustice, there will be resistance.

The Legacy of the L.A. 8: A Chronicle of Resistance

The L.A. 8 case was not just a legal battle; it was a defining moment for civil rights, political freedom, and dissent in the U.S. Over two decades, it tested justice, exposing the government's efforts to silence those who challenged its foreign policy.

This case reshaped the legal and political landscape for immigrant rights. It's not just a story, it's a historical record of resilience. It's a testament to defiance and an unwavering fight against political persecution.

This book is not meant to be an exhaustive record of our struggle; no pages could hold the full weight of those twenty years. What began as a case file grew into a lifetime; what was meant to break us became the measure of our endurance. For two decades, we lived in defiance, breathing under siege, holding fast to dignity when freedom itself was uncertain.

Ours was the longest immigration deportation case in U.S. history, but it was also something greater: a testament to the human will to stand upright when the world demands that you bow.

This is our story. Our victory.

The legacy we leave behind is not only in the legal briefs, the court rulings, or the headlines; it lives in the hearts of those who refused to surrender. It is a reminder that justice does not descend from power; it rises from persistence. That truth, no matter how long it is buried, will one day surface to breathe again.

We stood our ground, and we prevailed.

And if history remembers anything about the L.A. Eight,
let it remember this:

that we spoke when silence was safer,
stood when surrender was easier,
and believed, in the face of fear,
that justice belongs to those who refuse to be silenced.

What began with a knock meant to silence us
ended with a voice that could not be silenced.

ABOUT THE AUTHOR

Michel Shehadeh is a Palestinian-American writer, activist, and former civil rights defendant in one of the longest political deportation cases in U.S. history. He immigrated to the United States in 1975 to pursue higher education. His life took a dramatic turn when he was arrested by the U.S. government as part of the Los Angeles Eight case, a prosecution targeting Palestinian students and activists for their political views. After a twenty-year legal struggle, the case ended in a landmark civil-rights victory; in 2007, a federal judge dismissed the charges, calling the proceedings "an embarrassment to the rule of law."

Determined to complete his education despite years of legal persecution, Shehadeh earned a B.A. in Journalism and a master's degree in Public Administration from California State University, Long Beach. He later served as Western Regional Director of the American-Arab Anti-Discrimination Committee (ADC) and as Executive Director of the Arab Film Festival (AFF) in San Francisco.

A prolific writer in both English and Arabic, Shehadeh's work has appeared in The New York Times, Los Angeles Times, San Francisco Chronicle, The Bend Bulletin, Middle East Eye, Rai al-Youm, Al Mayadeen Net, and Al-Adab Magazine, among others.

Shehadeh lives in Bend, Oregon. He is married, has two sons, and is a grandfather of three.